DENNIS BRAIN

A Biography

DENNIS BRAIN

A Biography by
STEPHEN PETTITT

With an Appreciation by
BENJAMIN BRITTEN

ROBERT HALE · LONDON

Printed in Great Britain by
Clarke, Doble & Brendon Ltd,
Plymouth

Contents

Illustrations

Dennis Brain (1921–1957)*
by BENJAMIN BRITTEN, O.M., C.H.

Since the war, the horn playing of Dennis Brain has been one of the most familiar, certainly one of the happiest, features of British musical life. No season went by without his superlative performances as soloist in horn concertos. He was frequently to be seen at the first desk of one or other of the London orchestras, and no one will ever forget his inimitable tone and phrasing in the solo passages, from the small fragments in the works of the earlier masters (often devastatingly high—but so securely played), to the full dress melodies of more recent times (including Siegfried's horn call). Then there were his many appearances in chamber music either with a piano (Schumann's *Adagio and Allegro*, op. 70) or a string group (Mozart's Quintet, K 407). His own excellent ensemble, too, has delighted us with musicianly and beautifully rehearsed performances of music from Mozart to the present day, some of which was inspired by and written for Dennis.

The tragic car accident of 1st September leaves a musical gap which can never be filled. It has robbed us of an artist with the unique combination of a superb technical command of his instrument, great musicianship, a lively and intelligent interest in music of all sorts, and a fine performing temperament, coupled with a charming personality. It has also robbed us of a man of rare generosity, simplicity and charm.

I first met Dennis in the early summer of 1942. I was writing incidental music for a series of radio commentaries on war-time England which were being broadcast weekly to America at the ungodly hour of 3 am. The orchestra was that of the RAF, in which he was the first horn. I well remember being approached

* Reproduced from *Tempo* magazine No. 46, winter 1957–8, by kind permission of the author and editor.

by him at one of the rehearsals, over, I think, some technical point in a solo passage. (Needless to say, having heard his playing in the first programme of the series I took every opportunity to write elaborate horn solos into each subsequent score!) We soon became friends, and it took him no time at all to persuade me to write a special work for him. This turned out to be the Serenade for tenor, horn and strings, the première of which he and Peter Pears gave in 1943. His help was invaluable in writing the work; but he was always most cautious in advising any alterations. Passages which seemed impossible even for his prodigious gifts were practised over and over again before any modifications were suggested, such was his respect for a composer's ideas. He of course performed the work on many occasions, and for a period it seemed that no one else would ever be able to play it adequately. But, as usually happens when there is a work to play and a master who can play it, others slowly develop the means of playing it too, through his example. I must be grateful to Dennis for having challenged all other horn players in his playing of this piece. Some of my happiest musical experiences were conducting this work for him and Peter Pears—a succession of wonderful performances progressing from the youthful exuberance and brilliance of the early days to the maturity and deep understanding of the last few years.

Later, in 1954, I wrote another piece for Dennis, again with tenor, but this time with piano accompaniment, in memory of Noel Mewton-Wood. Noel was a close friend of all of us, and had given many recitals with Dennis. His death was equally tragic and unexpected. (One is left aghast when one thinks of the loss sustained by English music in these two deaths and that of Kathleen Ferrier, all young artists at the beginning of dazzling careers, in the space of only four years.) This time the work was a subdued *Canticle* (my third), the setting of a tragic poem of Edith Sitwell, and from the start Dennis understood the remote, elegiac mood. I shall never forget his playing of the dark opening, the slithering chromatic scales, or the thunderous low notes.

He came many times to play for us at the Aldeburgh Festival, but last June he came primarily to conduct. Here again he showed many of the same fine characteristics—musicianship, intelligence, enterprise and hard work—and one felt that his conducting would soon possess the same ease and persuasion of his horn playing. However, what one remembers most clearly of that evening was not his conducting, but his playing in this same concert of the unfinished movement of Mozart's fragmentary horn Concerto in E. The *tutti* started with its glorious richness. Delicate phrases followed with warm and intense counterpoint; brilliant passages for the violins, soothing oboe melodies. Then the solo entered—firm, heroic, and all seemed set for the best of all the wonderful Mozart horn concertos. And then suddenly in the middle of an intricate florid passage, superbly played, it stopped: silence. Dennis shrugged his shoulders and walked off the Jubilee Hall platform. That night, as always, he drove back home to London after the performance. Aldeburgh is not so far from London as Edinburgh, but far enough after a heavy day of rehearsals and performances, both conducting and playing. One protested, one always did, but off he went laughing. That was the last time I ever heard him play, the last time I saw him. That Mozart fragment sticks in my mind as a symbol of Dennis's own life. But it is not so easy for us to shrug our shoulders.

Preface

This book has been a labour of love. My own initial enthusiasm
met with an amazing, overwhelming response from all whom I
approached and without their continuing encouragement and un-
failing generosity none of this would have appeared in print. To
all who have helped in any way I am deeply grateful.

There is not room, alas, to mention them all. I must however
thank Denis Matthews for allowing me unlimited access not just
to his extensive library but also to his apparently inexhaustible
memory and for his supremely helpful comments on the text.
Many individuals gave me hours of their precious time, especially
Yvonne Brain and the late Leonard Brain, Hugh Bean, Jack
Brymer, Mrs Irene Burden, Walter Legge, Gareth Morris, Wilfred
Parry and Frank Probyn; Miss Mary Hodgson, her successors and
colleagues at the BBC Written Archives Centre spent hours of
research on my behalf; Mrs Alfred Brain and Bruce Craig un-
earthed a wealth of material from California; the record companies, in particular Decca and EMI, have been most helpful in
the preparation of the discography, as has Arthur Ridgewell of
the Sir Thomas Beecham Society; two close friends, Dr Norman
Macdougall and Martin Prowse, have proved invaluable in supply-
ing and cross-checking information.

Several composers readily supplied information on their particular association with Dennis Brain, notably Malcolm Arnold,
Peter Racine Fricker, Gordon Jacob and Ernest Tomlinson. I am
especially indebted to Benjamin Britten for offering as his personal
contribution to this book a tribute he first penned in the autumn
of 1957 in memory of an artist for whom he felt a deep respect
and affection and with whom he so often collaborated.

Finally I must thank Margaret, my wife, who has borne the in-
cessant clatter of the typewriter with amazing patience and who
has been a constant source of encouragement.

Stephen Pettitt

Newcastle upon Tyne September 1976

Early Days

Dennis Brain was the youngest in a family of horn-players. His father, two uncles and grandfather all achieved eminence on the instrument—a remarkable illustration of the inheritability of musical gifts. Even more remarkably, these gifts were improved upon with each succeeding generation until in Dennis they assumed the proportions of genius. While the main concern of this book must be with Dennis himself it would be wrong to neglect his predecessors and the part they played in shaping his destiny. Their close association with the origins and growth of many of our major symphony orchestras created the structure within which outstanding talent could arise. Opportunity for the expression of such talent was more than once the outcome of quite unforeseen events and circumstances.

So it is that we must look first at the careers of Dennis's grandfather, A. E. Brain, his uncles Arthur and Alfred, and his father Aubrey, observing at the same time the evolution of the instrument on which they had such a lasting influence.

The French horn is still held by some to be one of the most perilous instruments to play, a view which does much to enhance the prestige of any who have succeeded in taming this most intractable of orchestral animals! The late Anton Horner, horn-player and teacher of Philadelphia, once commented philosophically, "God makes some people horn-players; others are less fortunate." It is a fact that a certain degree of respect is extended to anyone embarking on a horn-playing career; but from those who have reached the top—and today there are many good players who have—the highest possible standards of execution and artistry are expected, no less than from a pianist or violinist.

On reflection this is a remarkable fact. Only thirty or forty years ago solo performances on the horn were rare and were listened to with nervous anticipation of the inevitable 'fluffs' and 'cracked' notes. This was equally true of the notorious horn solos in the orchestral repertoire. That we take today's high standards for granted is a result almost entirely of the career of one man— Dennis Brain—who in the space of only twenty years persuaded the public to accept the horn as a significant solo instrument, restored to the concert platform the Mozart and Haydn concertos which had long gathered the dust of infrequent use, and inspired most of the leading composers of the day to add significant solo works to the limited repertoire of his instrument. Perhaps most important of all, he showed that 'it could be done', that 'cracks' and 'bubbles' were things of the past. As Josef Eger rightly pointed out, "The four-minute mile for hornists has been breached. The magnificent Dennis Brain set the pace and now the horn is being featured as a solo instrument ever more widely. Once the four-minute mile was cracked by one human being, others felt that they could do it, too. They did so quickly and in numbers."*

The story of the horn's development as a serious musical instrument is comparatively brief. It did not appear in the orchestra until the early 1700s and only then on sufferance. It was loud and considered coarse in comparison with the violin and oboe.

Harmonic series for the horn in F

Furthermore, it could only produce about fifteen or sixteen notes over a compass of three octaves derived from a fundamental note, determined by the length of the tubing.

Of these notes, known as the 'harmonic series', about one third are slightly out of tune compared with the corresponding notes

* In "Breaking the Endurance Barrier", *Woodwind World*, May 1958.

of the tempered scale. The result was that the orchestral player was limited to less than a dozen notes that he could play in any one key. Despite these limitations the horn became an integral part of the orchestra and was probably first heard as such in Hamburg in 1705 when Keiser's opera *Octavia* was directed by Handel. England first heard the orchestral horn in Handel's own opera *Radamisto* at the Haymarket Theatre, London. It appeared in France in 1735 by which time the 'crook' system had been developed whereby tubes of differing lengths could be added to put the horn into a variety of keys.

The basic shape of the modern horn probably derives from the French (hence 'French' horn), who developed the ancient hunting horn into the *trompe de chasse*. Its coiled shape made it convenient to hold and the flared end, or bell, increased its carrying power and gave a resonance to its tone. Many perferred to call this resonance raucousness, and it was while trying to modify this that the Dresden player Hampel found, in about 1760, that the blatant sound could be softened by inserting the hand part-way into the bell. More significantly, he discovered that if the hand were pushed still further in, the pitch of the horn could be lowered by a semitone, then by a tone. The importance of this discovery was that the player was now able to fill in the 'gaps' between the natural notes of the harmonic series. A glance at the Figure will show that above the fourth harmonic the largest interval between any two harmonics is a major third, and therefore by using the hand it is possible to play a complete scale from C to C (fourth to eighth harmonics). The 'stopped' notes were of an inferior quality because the presence of the hand muffled them, but they were quite audible and reasonable intonation was possible.

Even if the hand were used, the horn was still limited to the notes of the key in which it was 'crooked'. It was not until 1818 that valves were patented: these were lengths of tubing which lowered the pitch of the horn by one, two or three semitones. With three valves fitted, seven different harmonic series were available, this being the maximum possible number of ways of combining the valves. Using all these, plus the notes obtainable naturally, it was now possible to play a complete chromatic scale with no perceptible loss of tone quality throughout the entire compass. However it was not until the middle of the nineteenth

century that the valve was mechanically perfected and almost
the end before it was accepted by the horn-playing world at large.
Players were suspicious, for they believed that the intrinsic beauty
of the horn's tone quality lay in its characteristic tapered shape,
and that valves, being cylindrical, would detract from this quality;
they preferred the hand horn, with all its limitations. Certainly
during the period between 1770 and 1830 many notable players
were trained in the hand-horn technique; they founded a school
of playing which determined the pattern of development throughout Europe for nearly another century. This Austro-Bohemian
tradition numbered among its adherents such players as Leutgeb,
for whom Mozart wrote his concertos and quintet, Punto, the
dedicatee of Beethoven's Sonata op. 17, Gallay, Dauprat and
Puzzi.

The Austro-Bohemian tradition exerted its influence on nearly
every horn-playing country. France, Germany, Italy were all
affected either directly, by the influx of players who then taught
in their own traditions, or indirectly, by the visits of Bohemian
hand-horn virtuosi. The influence was one of technique rather
than of tone; each country followed its own inclinations on the
latter count. The French preferred a horn with a narrow bore
expanding to a small bell, giving a bright, thin sound; the German
horns rapidly expanded to a large bell, while the Austrians com-
promised with a narrower bore and a large bell.

English horn-playing in the mid-1800s was also a by-product
of the Austro-Bohemian tradition. Handel had used Bohemian
players for his operatic productions over a hundred years earlier
and their influence remained. But the foundations of a truly
English style were laid by the brothers Joseph and Peter Petrides,
Bohemians who settled in England in 1802, and Giovanni Puzzi,
an Italian trained by Belloli in the Bohemian tradition, who also
settled in England in 1817. All three players used French Raoux
horns, noted for their clarity of tone; this factor, combined with
their Bohemian training, produced a beautiful and distinctive
sound which made the best of all possible worlds and was to reach
its climax very much later in the playing of Dennis Brain. There
were other players at the time in England—Tully, Jarrett, Holmes,
Harper—but they did not have the influence of Puzzi or the Petrides brothers, who were excellent teachers as well as performers.

Even after the arrival of such eminent players there were comparatively few opportunities for the public to hear them. The only regular orchestras were to be found attached to the theatres or the opera. There were, however, regular winter concerts in the St James's Hall given by the Philharmonic Society. This organization had been set up in 1813 for "the encouragement of orchestral and instrumental music"; it had no permanent orchestra but engaged the best players available when one was needed. There were frequent recitals of chamber music—one of the most popular works was the Beethoven Septet op. 20, played no less than twelve times in as many years. The Petrides brothers appeared regularly in the Society's concerts until their retirement in 1825. Then Puzzi became the principal player, taking part not only in chamber works but in lesser known horn concertos by Belloli and Costa. He was something of a composer himself and performed his own Concertante for horn a number of times.

But orchestral performances were still rare. For the average player symphony concerts took first place artistically but second place financially. Day-to-day expenses were met by earnings from playing in theatres, restaurants and music-halls.

Such was the position when in 1879 there arrived in England Friedrich Adolf Borsdorf, to take up a post with the stage band at Covent Garden. Born in Saxony in 1854, he had studied under Lorenz and Oscar Franz and served in a military band before he was offered the Covent Garden appointment by Hans Richter. He was joined in 1882 by a fellow-German, Franz Paersch, and together the two players added a new impetus to the development of English horn-playing. They had been trained on wide-bore German instruments but changed to French Raoux models on arrival in England; the combination of the broad German approach and the clarity of the French tone was something they were able to instil into the majority of their pupils. Borsdorf, in particular, was a prolific teacher; he was appointed professor at the Royal College of Music in 1882 and at the Royal Academy in 1897. He also quickly became the leading London horn-player; Richter frequently used him for his concerts as third horn, with Paersch as first horn. Then, when Paersch went north to join the Hallé Orchestra Borsdorf became Richter's principal player. Richter himself was a former horn-player at the Vienna Conservatory,

B

having come to England in May 1877 to conduct a series of Wagner concerts at the Royal Albert Hall. Borsdorf also played for the Philharmonic Society and for 'Clinton's Wind Quintet' which gave regular recitals at the Steinway Hall.

On 25 November 1893 there was opened in London a new concert hall that was to remain dear to the public's heart for nearly fifty years—the Queen's Hall in Langham Place. An inaugural concert was held on 2 December and from 28 February 1894 it became the new home of the Philharmonic Society's concerts. A year later Robert Newman, the manager of the hall, put to a young conductor, Henry Wood, the idea of holding 'Promenade' concerts in the Queen's Hall with a permanent orchestra. Wood approved wholeheartedly and on 10 August 1895 the first 'Prom' took place, with an orchestra of eighty players, led by Frye Parker.

First horn was Adolf Borsdorf; the fourth horn was a Mr A. E. Brain, late of the Scots Guards, and first of three generations of horn-players known in later years to the profession as the 'Brain Trust'.

Alfred Edwin Brain was born on 4 February 1860 at Turnham Green, London, the only son of William Brain, who had been invalided out of the Crimean War and lived as a Chelsea Pensioner in the Militia Stores. Alfred received very little formal education and at the age of twelve enlisted in the Scots Guards as Band Boy, where he played the horn. In a service career of eighteen and a half years he succeeded in rising to the rank of corporal; he left the Guards on 30 April 1891 to seek civilian employment as a musician and was thus only entitled to a modified pension.

In 1880 he had married Letitia Fearn, a woman of strong character and a devoted companion. No one could have described her as beautiful; her very stature made her imposing, almost overbearing, as did the rather masculine outlines of her head and face. Nevertheless, the firm line of her jaw, well-formed facial muscles and high cheekbones added a handsome dignity to her simple, kindly nature. It was from her that later members of the Brain family derived the anatomical foundations of their ability to play the horn.

Letitia and Alfred had seven children, not all of whom had

remarkable musical abilities. Of the four boys, Hugh became a captain in the American Merchant Marine and Arthur, the youngest child, after only a very few years as a professional horn-player, retired and joined the City of London Police. Two of the girls played stringed instruments, Letitia the violin and Rebecca the 'cello, neither with outstanding brilliance. Helena, however, was a very competent player of the long F trumpet, popular at the time. At a concert given in Reading in May 1899 by Mrs Arkwright, founder of the English Ladies Orchestral Society, Helena was engaged as principal trumpet while her father played principal horn. A. E. Brain, in fact, appeared many times as soloist in the Newbury Amateur Orchestral Union; the programmes included works such as the Beethoven op. 81b Sextet for two horns and strings, which has very difficult parts for both horns, and the Brahms op. 40 Horn Trio, so he cannot have been too bad a player. Both the remaining boys, Alfred and Aubrey, showed early musical promise and were to become outstanding performers on the horn.

A. E. Brain (senior), as father came to be known, also played for the Philharmonic Society from 1894, usually as fourth horn, except for two seasons between 1897 and 1899, when he alternated between second and third. Like many others he supplemented his concert engagements with theatre and restaurant work—again as fourth horn. In fact he played fourth horn so frequently that he became known affectionately as 'George IV'. To play in this position carried no stigma. Admittedly, his years as a bandsman had given little style or musicality to his playing, but he was a substantial and reliable player and could blend his tone easily with others. The horn quartets of the Queen's Hall, the Philharmonic Society and later the London Symphony Orchestra and Covent Garden all owed something of their perfection of ensemble to this bluff ex-Guardsman.

The early Prom programmes in which A. E. Brain played were a quaint mixture compared with those of today. There were many more items, and they tended to feature short solos rather than lengthy symphonic works. There was always a fantasia on themes from various operas and operettas in which the various principals of the orchestra were highlighted. One significant orchestral item to be found in the 1903 prospectus is the Mozart Sinfonia Concertante K 297b for oboe, clarinet, horn and bassoon. This is a lengthy work with a soloistic horn part. Adolf Borsdorf was joined by D. Lalande (oboe), M. Gomez (clarinet) and E. F. James (bassoon).

Because he had received very little formal musical training himself, A. E. Brain ensured that those of his children who showed any musical promise were offered the best opportunities available. His eldest son, Alfred, born on 24 October 1885 and also given the second name of Edwin, started to learn the trumpet at the age of six. He was presumably influenced to some extent by his sister Helena, but when he was twelve he decided to change to the horn and for four years was taught by his father. Alfred's schooling was completed at grammar school which he left at the age of sixteen. Then, in February 1901, he won a scholarship to the Royal Academy of Music to study the horn with Adolf Borsdorf. At the Academy he also learned the piano with G. D. Cunningham (who was to teach Dennis organ nearly forty years later) and harmony with J. McEwen. When Alfred left the Royal Academy in June 1904 he had gained both silver and bronze medals for horn-playing and a certificate of merit for piano.

In that same month came a significant development in London's orchestral history—the birth of the London Symphony Orchestra. It was the immediate product of a clash between Henry Wood and the 'deputy system' as it affected his own Queen's Hall Orchestra. Frequently Queen's Hall rehearsals were scheduled for the same days as other, more lucrative engagements, and players therefore employed deputies to cover the occasional rehearsals they could not attend, paying them a smaller fee and pocketing the difference. Many players used very little discretion in this matter; the result was that many rehearsals, and indeed concerts, took place with orchestras three quarters of whose players might be deputies. The system annoyed Henry Wood more than most and his exasperation can be illustrated by the well-known story of the double-bass player who, on being congratulated by Wood for attending all the rehearsals, confessed that he would unfortunately not be able to attend the concert itself!

Borsdorf himself was once the victim of Henry Wood's anger. One night Wood was conducting a Wagner programme at Queen's

Hall and looked up to find Borsdorf missing. It came to him in a flash where he was. At the interval, therefore, he told Robert Newman to hold things up for a few minutes, jumped into a cab and went as fast as possible round to the St James's Hall. There, as anticipated, he found Borsdorf playing for Richter. Creeping behind him Wood grabbed Borsdorf by the collar, whispered into his startled ear "You're coming with me," led him firmly to the cab and had him back in the Queen's Hall before the second half of the programme was due to begin! Amusing incidents in retrospect, but their constant repetition made the whole deputy system very annoying.

So on 30 September 1903 Henry Wood struck out. His manager, Robert Newman, appeared on the platform at the beginning of the morning rehearsal with the brief announcement that from that day each player was to receive a flat rate of £100 per annum—provided that Queen's Hall had first call on his services. There were to be no more deputies.

Forty-six players immediately resigned, including three of the horns—Borsdorf, Van der Meerschen and Busby. Busby proposed that a new orchestra be formed and before long a working committee consisting of Borsdorf, Busby (chairman), Van der Meerschen, J. R. Solomon (trumpet), A. Hobday (double-bass) and E. F. James (bassoon) was set up to recruit players. In addition to the original forty-six, many more came from the Queen's Hall Orchestra, including A. E. Brain, who thus completed the horn quartet. Hans Richter agreed to conduct the first concert, which took place on the afternoon of 9 June 1904 with an orchestra numbering ninety-nine players, led by Arthur Payne. Among those in the audience in Queen's Hall to witness this historic event was Henry Wood. He held no resentment; it was simply a matter of principle.

The London Symphony Orchestra made an enormous impact not just as a body but by virtue of its constituent sections. The horn quartet—Borsdorf, Busby, Van der Meerschen, A. E. Brain—was particularly fine. Edric Cundell, who studied the horn himself under the 'rough but sound' tuition of Thomas Busby, wrote that he never heard a horn quartet equal to that of the LSO—irreverently known as 'God's Own Quartet'. "As a chorus," he wrote, "the four stayed together as far as humanly possible and made a real and unforgettable blend of tone, playing into each other's style and personality until ensemble became a true unity of effort." His ability to blend with others was A. E. Brain's chief asset as a player and he sustained this talent whether in the LSO or in the smallest 'pit' orchestra. He had extended his work to Covent Garden where as fourth to Paersch, Baggs and Busby he played for several seasons under Richter. Many of the works in the LSO's library were given by the players themselves and A. E. Brain made his contribution—Beethoven's "Pastoral" Symphony.

In the autumn of 1904, while Henry Wood was struggling to patch up his decimated Queen's Hall Orchestra, Alfred obtained his first professional post, as third horn of the Scottish Orchestra in Glasgow. A 'seasonal body of eighty players', the Scottish Orchestra (the predecessor of today's Scottish National Orchestra) had been founded in 1893. Its chief attraction in those times was that it offered a three-month spell of regular paid concerts each winter. Guest conductors had included Wood, Richter and Richard Strauss. Two concerts per week were given in Glasgow, one in Edinburgh, and their standard was said to be even higher than that of the London Proms. The orchestra was the training-ground of many famous London players; its leaders included H. Verbrugghen and David MacCallum and a glance at the list of principals for the 1908–9 season alone reveals such names as A. Halstead, R. Waller, W. S. Hinchcliff, G. W. Anderson—all of whom later became prominent London players.

Alfred was appointed principal horn of the Scottish Orchestra for his second season and spent three years with them under the baton of their regular conductor, Sir Frederick Cowen. There were occasional opportunities for solo work such as the Mozart Sinfonia Concertante K 297b, in which he took part on 17 February 1906. Of the standard orchestral works there was one never-to-be-forgotten performance of the Beethoven "Choral" Symphony. To make room for the chorus the orchestra had to be squeezed into the middle of the platform. The tympanist, placed immediately above and behind Alfred, suddenly became ill in the middle of the performance and vomited—all over the back and shoulders of Alfred, who was not deterred from continuing and giving an impeccable, if uncomfortable, performance!

On 4 February 1908 Alfred gave a 'farewell' performance to

the Scottish Orchestra of the Romance and Finale from Mozart's Third Horn Concerto; he had been offered and accepted the post of principal horn of the Queen's Hall Orchestra. Henry Wood's rebuilt orchestra had been something of a disappointment and had to compete with the fabulous success of the new London Symphony Orchestra. During the winter of 1907–8 he started to look round for some players of a higher standard in an attempt to restore some of the Queen's Hall's former glory. With Alfred as principal horn Henry Wood soon had a fine horn quartet, almost on a par with that of the LSO. The other three players were Fred Salkeld, Oskar Borsdorf (Adolf's eldest son) and G. W. Smith.

Henry Wood now had further opportunity to introduce exciting new works into the Promenade concerts which of late had become somewhat stereotyped. On 8 October 1909 the horn quartet gave the first performance in England of Schumann's very difficult Konzertstück in F op. 86 for four horns and orchestra. This can have been no mean feat on the narrow-bore piston-valved instrument then in use, and the work was not heard again in England until April 1971. London audiences also heard for the first time Bach's Brandenburg Concerto no. 1 on 28 November 1908 (with Alfred Brain and Fred Salkeld) and the Beethoven Sextet op. 81b for two horns and strings on 10 September 1909.

Alfred's personality as a young man was a mixture of kindliness and extreme bluntness. Always ready to help young players to make a start in the profession he could be very ruthless in obtaining that end. When Frank Probyn came to London in 1910 to try for entry to the Royal College of Music Alfred offered to put him up, giving him his address in Shepherd's Bush. Probyn found the address, only to discover the house empty and to be told that the Brains had moved that day to Acton. When he arrived at Acton, the house was in chaos, with packing-cases everywhere. He was invited in by Alfred's wife and made to sit down while she carried on unpacking. She was Jewish, an ex-Tiller girl, who, after her marriage to Alfred, clung to him as persistently as he tried to avoid her. Probyn got a taste of their stormy relationship when Alfred came home later that evening; he heard language fly from both of them such as he had never heard before. Alfred, in his blunt and profane way, insisted that 'the boy' be given a good meal and allowed to get to bed.

Alfred also ensured that Probyn was given every opportunity during his student days to gain horn-playing experience. He made him his deputy at the Shaftesbury Theatre where he was first horn. The conductor, Arthur Wood, also looked after Probyn, who was coolly received by the older members of the orchestra; they showed strong disapproval of up-and-coming provincials. Probyn was able to return the kindnesses shown him by Alfred by acting as his scribe, since Alfred found great difficulty in composing and writing letters. One such letter was to the Queen's Hall Orchestra to ask for a higher fee.

A. E. Brain (senior) kept a firm watch over Alfred with the same mixture of bluntness and kindliness, especially when his actions affected others. On one occasion Alfred had sent Probyn to deputize for him at a concert in Winchester Cathedral so that he could spend the day at the Orchestral Association playing cards, as he frequently did. That evening 'Papa' Brain came round to the house. "What the . . . did you mean by sending the youngster to Winchester?" He told Probyn that for his own good he should not stay in Alfred's home any longer. Not long afterwards, Alfred himself also left the house, and his wife, and moved to Elstree, where close friends, Tom Gutteridge the trombonist and his wife, ran a pub.

The Queen's Hall Orchestra had a succession of notable visiting conductors though their permanent conductor remained Henry Wood, for whom all the players had warm respect and admiration. There were, however, occasional rows. When Wood introduced Bartók's Suite for Orchestra for the first time, Alfred rose from his seat to ask:

"Surely you can find better novelties than this?" Alfred was already the 'shop steward' of the orchestra. Wood's reply emphasized the give-and-take atmosphere of the orchestra.

"I have to interpret all schools of music—much that I don't really care for!"

There were also humorous occasions, such as the time someone locked Alfred in the lavatory just before a concert. The conductor's attention was divided between keeping the orchestra together and looking anxiously at the empty first horn chair. Suddenly Alfred appeared just in time to play his solo, hair dishevelled and minus his collar and tie, having escaped by climbing out of the window and down a drain-pipe!

During his early professional career Alfred played on a Courtois two-valve horn which he had picked up cheaply in a junk shop. He added a third valve and with his small mouthpiece produced a sound that thrilled many; especially when he played quietly, his sound seemed to float from nowhere, and some people still recall his performances not only of the Schumann and Bach works already mentioned but also of Strauss's First Horn Concerto. He had the physical advantages of the 'Brain' facial bone and jaw structure—wide palate and small teeth—features he inherited from his mother. As a pupil of Borsdorf he had learnt to use a great deal of pressure, but his physical strength prevented him from tiring easily as a result. During the pre-1914 days in the Queen's Hall Orchestra, when he spent many hours after rehearsals drinking and playing cards, Alfred could not always be relied upon, and after a heavy night he might make some really appalling 'fluffs'. He was never insensitive to his own weaknesses, however. He found considerable difficulty with the lower notes on the horn and never trusted himself to play the last two notes of the famous *Till Eulenspiegel* theme. They were left to the second horn.

Alfred also possessed a very fine, light tenor voice and at the outbreak of the war in 1914 was considering taking up singing seriously. Encouragement had come from no less a person than Sir Thomas Beecham, but the war brushed aside this ambition.

Although Alfred was gaining widespread recognition as a horn-player of no mean ability, the leading London player was still his old teacher, Adolf Borsdorf. Borsdorf had in fact in 1896 taken part in the first performance in England, at the Crystal Palace, of *Till Eulenspiegel*, with Strauss himself conducting. He had been absent from the first rehearsal and the other members of the orchestra had laid bets that he would 'split' the opening solo. They lost their bets. Borsdorf's reputation was such that Elgar often consulted him about the suitability of certain horn passages in new works. He was also a member of King Edward VII's private band, one of a group of London Symphony Orchestra players known grandly as 'Musicians in Ordinary, under Royal Warrant to the King'.

In March 1911 Richter returned to Germany and for a while

Elgar became conductor of the LSO. He was soon replaced by Nikisch, whose ability with orchestras was legendary. It was he who had first brought Tchaikovsky's Fifth Symphony to England in 1895, and he had lost no time in introducing it to the LSO. When he first rehearsed it, he fixed his eyes on Borsdorf as he started the long solo at the opening of the slow movement; the beauty of Borsdorf's playing so affected Nikisch that he dropped his baton. With a mumbled apology he said, "Beautiful—but let us do it again, Mr Borsdorf." The second version was even better than the first; in the pubs afterwards it was maliciously suggested that, away from Nikisch, Borsdorf could not have phrased the solo with the same nuances to save his life.

Early in 1912 Howard Pew, a New York concert agent, succeeded in persuading Nikisch to tour the USA (with a brief excursion into Canada) with an orchestra of his own choice. Without hesitation Nikisch chose the London Symphony Orchestra. It was the first tour of the USA by a British orchestra and a total of one hundred players, plus librarian and porter, was engaged and booked on the *Titanic*. Four complete programmes were compiled and meticulously rehearsed and twenty-eight concerts booked in cities ranging from Ottawa to Kansas, from Washington to Milwaukee. Fortunately for both the LSO and posterity a change of schedule forced the agent to alter the booking from the *Titanic* to the *Baltic*; on the fateful night of 14 April as the *Titanic* went to the bottom the LSO was in Cleveland, Ohio, performing (appropriately) Tchaikovsky's "Pathétique" Symphony.

Many of the American critics thought the "brasses excellent" and spoke very highly of the whole orchestra. It is interesting to compare two reviews of the same concert, in Symphony Hall, Boston. First the *Boston Herald*:

The brass is in no way remarkable; on the contrary, the horns were uncertain and thrumpets [*sic*] and trombones were often coarse and blatant.

While the Boston *Christian Science Monitor* commented:

A collective conception results in those perfectly adjusted string and brass sections of the LSO. . . .

A. E. Brain (senior) was unable to go on the tour as he was under contract to Covent Garden. In his place Borsdorf chose Alfred's younger brother, Aubrey, then only eighteen years old and principal horn of the New Symphony Orchestra.

Aubrey, born on 12 July 1893, had also taken up music at an early age, but his first instrument was the violin. As soon as he was able he learnt to play the horn and, like Alfred, was first taught by his father. His musical grounding was completed by lessons from Adela Sutcliffe and Eugene Mieir, and by the time he was seventeen he won a scholarship to the Royal College of Music. He studied the horn under Borsdorf as an Open Foundation scholar from May 1911 to April 1913, winning great admiration for his playing from many of the prominent conductors of the day. Both he and Leon Goossens, the oboist, played in the North London Orchestral Society in their student days. Sir Charles Stanford, the composer who also taught composition at the Royal College of Music, noted a certain narrowness of outlook in Aubrey's personality. "I want more than just a good horn-player," he observed. This aspect of Aubrey's character was in marked contrast to his brother Alfred's extrovert, if less refined, personality. Landon Ronald, conductor of the New Symphony Orchestra, was less concerned with personal qualities and late in 1911 made Aubrey his first horn. Ronald had been permanent conductor of the orchestra since 1909, when Beecham had relinquished the post after three years spent establishing it with series of Queen's Hall and provincial concerts. There were some excellent players—Eli Hudson (flute), Charles Draper (clarinet) and John Saunders, the leader. The horns included a Mr Muskett and a Mr Button; eighteen-year-old Aubrey suffered a cool reception from the older players, but he quickly won praise for the quality and purity of his playing.

Aubrey returned from his trip to the States to join both his father and brother in the Royal Albert Hall *Titanic* Memorial Concert on 24 May 1912. No less than twenty-four horn-players formed part of the largest orchestra ever assembled in the Royal Albert Hall. The programme included excerpts from Tchaikovsky's "Pathétique" Symphony, Elgar's Enigma Variations, and Sullivan's Overture "In Memoriam".

Talented though he undoubtedly was, Aubrey was ever aware of the shadow cast both by his elder brother Alfred and by Adolf Borsdorf. There was simply not enough work at that time to keep three leading players fully occupied. The New Symphony was a good orchestra, but it was not in the same class as the Queen's Hall or the London Symphony, nor did it provide an adequate livelihood for a young man. When, in the autumn of 1913, Beecham rescued the Denhof Opera Company from a financially disastrous provincial tour and offered Aubrey the post of principal horn of the new Beecham Opera Company, Aubrey jumped at the opportunity. The position meant a spell of regular paid work outside London with an orchestra of players drawn from Covent Garden, the LSO, the Queen's Hall and the Beecham Symphony Orchestra. It also offered wide experience of playing to a young musician; the seventeen-week tour had a repertoire that included (all in English) Wagner's *Ring, Tristan and Isolde, The Master Singers, The Flying Dutchman, Tannhaüser,* as well as *Elektra, Der Rosenkavalier, The Magic Flute, Orpheus* and *Pelléas and Mélisande.*

Aubrey found the Beecham Opera Company tour more than just musically rewarding. One of the company's principals was a mezzo-soprano named Marion Beeley. Born in Stalybridge, the daughter of an engineer from Hyde, she had first sung in the Rosemount Methodist Church in Hyde where her uncle, Thomas Carter Beeley, was the organist and choirmaster. He encouraged and assisted her in her musical education; she sang in a number of concerts and oratorio performances in the Manchester area before she went to London to join the Covent Garden Company, where she sang in the chorus and in minor solo roles. She appeared twice at the Proms in August 1912, and Beecham then chose her as one of the principals for the September 1913 tour. It was not long before she and Aubrey met and the tour marked the beginning of a whirlwind courtship. They were engaged soon after and married in the summer of 1914, just before the outbreak of war.

Though the Beecham tour had given Aubrey wider experience of the horn's repertoire it did not make his position in London any more secure. But one obstacle in the path of his success was soon removed. During the summer of 1913 Adolf Borsdorf had been taken ill with a severe attack of pyorrhoea and as a result had to have all his teeth removed. For a player who used a great deal of mouthpiece pressure this was disastrous; as soon as he was able to play again he moved to second horn in the London Symphony and Busby became principal. His place in the Royal Philharmonic was taken by Alfred Brain. But Borsdorf suffered a second and, psychologically, probably more damaging setback. He became the object of the growing anti-German feeling prevalent in the months preceding the First World War. He hotly maintained that he was a *Saxon*, not a *Prussian*, but popular feeling is not easily pacified by such subtle distinctions and Borsdorf was soon forced to resign.

The outbreak of war in 1914 marked the beginning of four very turbulent years in London's musical history, but it left the hierarchy of the horn-playing world firmly in the hands of the two Brain brothers, Alfred and Aubrey. Alfred now had ten years of top-rank playing behind him under some of the world's leading conductors. Aubrey had potentially the greater talent, but, still only twenty-one, he lacked the experience to support it and the personal drive to assert it. The war and its aftermath would decide the issue.

✅ 2 ✅

Uncle Alfred

As more and more musicians entered the armed services it became increasingly difficult to continue public concerts in London. The Covent Garden Opera House had been closed since the summer of 1914 and used as a store but the first victims of the war itself were the Proms which were suspended at the end of the 1915 season. The London Symphony Orchestra struggled on until early 1917 with some concerts conducted by Beecham and Henry Wood but it, too, had to suspend its activities for a while. Only the Royal Philharmonic Society continued, on a limited scale, to give concerts; Thomas Busby took over as first horn after the Brain brothers joined up.

Both Aubrey and Alfred joined the services, but in very different circumstances. Aubrey saw no action at all; although one periodical later described how "the young husband had to leave his wife and take his place manfully in defence of his Country and King" he in fact enlisted in the Welsh Guards on 24 February 1916 and remained with them until August 1920, playing the horn in the band. While he was in the Guards he bought his first car, a 1914 Singer, and started a lifelong interest in cars and motoring generally. Alfred joined the Scots Guards in November 1915 as soon as the Prom season was over and the Queen's Hall had closed. The last season had included Bach's Brandenburg Concerto no. 1 for the fifth time in almost as many years, and he had also played the horn obbligato in one of Tchaikovsky's songs, "Nay, Though my Heart Should Break".

In the Scots Guards Alfred was held on reserve until August 1916, when he was called up to be given training in communications. He was sent to the French front in May 1917 where he spent over a year in the hazardous work of stringing up the vital telephone cable links between battle stations. As he later recalled, the 'tremendous crashes of sound and the deep diapason of the siege artillery' were unforgettable. In July 1918 he was wounded in the right leg and hand by shrapnel and invalided out. For a while it was feared that his horn-playing days were over and that the hand would have to be amputated. Happily, he made a complete recovery and spent six months with the Army of Occupation in Cologne playing the horn again in the Coastguards band. He was awarded the British War Medal and Victory Medal for his gallantry and was given an honourable discharge on 6 May 1919, whereupon he hurried back to England to pick up the threads of musical life which were at last becoming somewhat less tenuous.

In London, Alfred found Sir Thomas Beecham already engaged in a summer season of opera at Covent Garden and with a lease on the theatre for the winter of 1919–20. Aubrey was still in service so Beecham appointed Alfred as first horn. His first engagement was in *Aïda*; his delight at being back inspired him to give of his energetic best that night—to such effect that he could not play again for a week. Nevertheless, he returned and played at Covent Garden for two more seasons with many famous conductors, among them Bruno Walter, who gave a *Ring* cycle, as well as Mancinelli, Campanini, Panizza and Emil Cooper. The early post-war years were a period of some insecurity for Covent Garden and opera generally. Beecham ran another summer season in 1920 but had to wind up his own Beecham Opera Company in October of that year. There followed a twelve-week experiment in the autumn, during which the Carl Rosa company was based at the Garden; the result was a complete financial disaster, and after much deliberation the British National Opera Company was formed. Its first performances were in Bradford in February 1922 and at Covent Garden (with *La Bohème*) in May.

Alfred's father, A. E. Brain (senior), returned to Covent Garden after the war as fourth horn. He also rejoined the Queen's Hall Orchestra (now known as the 'New' Queen's Hall Orchestra since the hall had been taken over by Chappells in 1915) and, with occasional theatre engagements at the People's Palace and elsewhere, this was all the playing he could now manage. He had left the London Symphony Orchestra in April 1916, and repeated bouts of bronchitis forced him to restrict his performances. He did

manage to play for the few concerts held each year by the Royal
Philharmonic Society.

Both the Queen's Hall and London Symphony Orchestras resumed full activities in the autumn of 1919. Alfred returned to
his post of principal horn at Queen's Hall, and early in this
first season Henry Wood took the opportunity of presenting the
first performance of Tcherepnin's Quartet for horns. Bach's
Brandenburg Concerto no. 1 made its first post-war appearance at
the Proms. Under the new administration, the Queen's Hall
Orchestra was run on a co-operative basis, each of one hundred
members holding ten shares of stock. In the London Symphony
Orchestra, Alfred started after the war as second horn and then
as co-principal with Van der Meerschen, since administrative work
took up more of the latter's time.

Such was the situation confronting Aubrey when he left the
Welsh Guards on 11 August 1920. His brother had resumed his
monopoly of the leading London orchestras and for two years the
best appointment he was able to obtain was as third horn for the
Royal Philharmonic Society. Aubrey needed work badly; Marion,
his wife, had given up a great deal of her singing work to bring
up their first son, Leonard, born in 1915. She still sang for Covent
Garden, though, and had made some records for HMV, but the
birth of a second son, Dennis, in 1921 meant that even more of
her time had to be spent at home. Aubrey could be sure of success
only if Alfred, with whom he was never on the best of terms, relinquished his monopoly of at least one of the big orchestras. And
Alfred, at the age of thirty-seven, was extremely unlikely to do anything of the sort. In fact he was expanding his musical interests. Together with R. Murchie (flute), Leon Goossens (oboe), Haydn
Draper (clarinet) and W. James (bassoon) he formed the London
Wind Quintet which made a number of records for Edison Bell in
1921–2. Though they were of rather obscure items such as the
Andante and Allegro by Scarlatti, *Pasacalle* by A. Barther and the
Quintet from Act Two of *Carmen*, they did much to promote interest in recorded wind music.

Two factors, however, brought about just the opening that
Aubrey required. Alfred's relations with his wife were, if anything,
worse after the war. Try as he might, she refused to be shaken off
and followed him doggedly wherever he went. She would even turn

up unexpectedly when he was playing a summer season at a seaside theatre, such as at the Spa at Bridlington in 1921. Escape by emigration was never far from his mind and, of all the possibilities, the USA offered the most attractions. The leading American orchestras contained large numbers of Europeans who had emigrated, and their representatives came yearly to London to attract and audition new members. The leading oboist of the Queen's Hall, de Busscher, had gone out to join the Los Angeles Philharmonic in 1913, thereby giving the young Leon Goossens his first big 'break' in orchestral playing. De Busscher had been followed by Emile Ferir (viola) and Alf Kastner (harp); the financial temptations of the USA, which had suffered less from the war, were undeniable.

When Walter Damrosch, conductor of the New York Symphony Orchestra, visited London during the winter of 1921–2 for a series of concerts at the Queen's and Royal Albert Halls he mentioned to Alfred that there was a vacancy in his orchestra. Alfred needed very little persuasion to take it; he remained in London for the remainder of the concert season and in late September 1922 sailed with his daughter, Olga, for the United States.

For one season, from 23 October 1922 until 20 March 1923, Al (as he became known to his American colleagues and friends) was co-principal of the New York Symphony with Santiago Richart. He also taught at the Juilliard School of Music in New York. Al drew up his own contract for the New York Symphony and it is reproduced here for its inherent interest.

SYMPHONY SOCIETY OF NEW YORK

1. I agree to play Horn for the Symphony Society of New York for the season of 1922–1923 beginning on or about October 23rd, 1923. The season shall consist of a minimum of thirty (30) consecutive weeks. The Symphony Society of New York has the privilege of further prolonging this season of thirty (30) weeks at its pleasure by notifying me of such extension on or before March 20th, 1923.

2. During the term of this contract, I agree to play to the best of my ability whenever called upon by the Symphony Society of New York in rehearsals, solo and public performances.

3. In case of war, strikes or force majeure the Symphony Society of New York has the right to cancel this contract.

c

4. For my services, as above specified, the Symphony Society of New York agrees to pay me the sum of one hundred dollars ($100.00) a week.

5. The Symphony Society of New York shall have the privilege of renewing this agreement under the same terms and conditions for the season of 1923–1924 by notifying me on or before April 1st, 1923.

6. All further details not specified in this agreement are to be arranged in accordance with the rules and by-laws of the New York Local, 802, A.F. of M.

Alfred Brain

Approved and accepted by the
SYMPHONY SOCIETY OF NEW YORK
Per *George Ingles*   Manager.

The Symphony Society of New York did not, however, have the privilege of renewing this agreement. Al was not yet happily settled; there was an uncomfortable rivalry between the New York Symphony and Philharmonic Orchestras which did not make Damrosch an easy man to work for. Nor was New York the American paradise painted for him by his old Queen's Hall colleagues. The money was good but the East Coast climate was not a sufficient improvement on what he had left behind. In the spring of 1923, therefore, he jumped at an offer to go to Los Angeles as principal horn of the Philharmonic Orchestra there. He bought a car and with Olga set out across the continent for the west. For the 1920s it was an enterprising venture and as Al said "a liberal education as to the vastness of this country and, taken all in all, a most delightful trip".

They arrived in Los Angeles in mid-September and Al lost no time in writing home to England to tell his family of his safe arrival. He received the following letter from his father:

1.9.23

My Dear Children

You will be sorry to hear Mother Past away on 31st July after long & terrible suffering in the end it was a Happy release: it was to her not to me she was a great Pall for forty years is a long time; but to me it is all too short but it is not for us to will but the great Ruler she was all the world to me.

I. was pleased to receive your letter this morning 1st Oct. that you had arrived it was rather daring thing to do going through a strange

country but glad you arrived quite safe you must have had a time
of it I envy you all that ride Poor Olga what experience for the
poor child she will never for that journey I hope you had good
weather we had a terrible month a August was thinking of you &
your journey all the time. you will be pleased to hear Aubrey had a
good success at the Proms he played the Mozart *Conto* got nice
notice in the times. Nellie & the children were over to London for
a month when Mother Past away Harry came for Funeral it was
good of him we had lots of letters condolance she is buried in the
Family grave at Brompton & the Minister from the hospital came &
read the service for her said she was one of the most patient
sufferers he had ever seen she was very much liked, all the hospital
staff got quite to like. Letitia & me was with her when died her
last were my best nurse is coming on at 8. I shall good Bath tonight
when she came she just smiled & went unconcies to the end

    Best love you your all

    loving dad

Letitia's death had clearly had a profound effect on his father,
and Al was deeply shocked, even though the news had not been
entirely unexpected.

It was some consolation for his domestic worries that Al undoubtedly found his new career infinitely rewarding. The Philharmonic was an excellent orchestra and gave regular concerts both
in Los Angeles itself and in the surrounding area. In addition there
were the annual summer concerts at the Hollywood Bowl, for
which the Philharmonic provided the orchestra. These alone were
lucrative enough, but gradually other outlets for his talents
presented themselves. As the Hollywood film industry expanded,
and with the advent of the 'talkies', increasing numbers of
musicians were needed to provide background music—in fact
film music became an industry in itself. Al played for the film
studios from 1927 until he retired, first for MGM and later for
Twentieth-Century Fox. He even appeared in the first Al Jolson
films.

Al maintained his links with England through more than family
letters. Arthur Bliss, Henry Wood and Eugene Goossens all
visited the States during the 1920s. Bliss came to Santa Barbara
in 1923 to conduct a performance of Mendelssohn's *Elijah* with
a good local choir and string orchestra. The wind players were
'imported' from Los Angeles, and Al was responsible for engag-

ing them. On the evening before the concert Bliss gave a dinner for the Los Angeles players, among whom he was delighted to find not only Al but other ex-London players he had known before the war. The evening was a very merry one; Al was an unofficial source of alcohol (these were prohibition days) and the supply was apparently endless. Bliss had a hangover the next day but Al was in his place for the performance, beaming all over his face and playing with complete confidence. There were almost equally merry reunions with Henry Wood in July 1926 and with Eugene Goossens in 1929, who both came to conduct at the Hollywood Bowl.

Although Al had been brought up strictly to play the narrow-bore French horn, once in the USA he soon changed to a wide-bore instrument. He had no interest in experimenting with countless permutations of instrument and mouthpiece. He knew exactly what he wanted—to retain the purity of tone for which he had been renowned in England and yet have an instrument that would cope with the heavy demands made upon it. Al had a five-valve Alexander horn made up for him by Sansone, the New York manufacturer, and used it almost exclusively for the rest of his career. It was basically a B♭ single horn with a thumb-valve change to A, and a little finger valve change to F for the lowest notes. An unusual feature was the mouthpipe, which could be changed; Al had three mouthpipes, one the Alexander pipe that came with the horn, the second a Conn pipe and the third made to his own specification. Thus with a narrow mouthpipe and a small mouthpiece Al could achieve the compromise he wanted—ease of playing but purity of sound. With five valves, he also had several valve combinations for each note, resulting in excellent intonation.

Such was Al's determination to make the USA his permanent home that he took out his first citizenship papers within a year of arriving in Los Angeles. Officially he was only on 'furlough' from the Queen's Hall and still held his shares, but his mind was made up and on 14 February 1930 he became a full US citizen. He found added security in finally divorcing his first wife. The marriage had never promised to be a happy one; Al's nature was admittedly easy-going but in the furtherance of his career he had to display a single-mindedness that did not suit his wife. In America he found the ideal companion who shared both his ambitions and his attitudes, and in 1932 he married 'Straussie'—a charming woman who had a zest for life and good-natured tolerance that helped to make them a devoted couple for the next thirty-four years. In their new-found happiness they made countless friends both in the music profession and in the community as a whole.

Al's increasing security and happiness were echoed in his professional life. Working both for the Philharmonic and for the Hollywood Bowl Orchestras he was extremely busy. He commanded respect for his integrity as much as for his expertise in horn-playing. He gave very few lessons—just some occasional private tuition—but his example and precepts influenced many of the leading players in the area. His artistry was matched only by his endurance; many was the time he would follow an evening Philharmonic concert with an all-night movie session, turning up for the next morning's rehearsal as if he had just spent eight hours in bed.

Al's début as a soloist with his own orchestra came on 22 August 1931 at the Hollywood Bowl (the last in the summer series) when Artur Rodzinski conducted. He played Strauss's First Concerto in a performance that was also heard by many thousands over the radio. Many wrote to express their appreciation, from the Bowl management to the humblest radio listener. There was some surprise that the Philharmonic had not seen fit to feature him as soloist before, but in America as much as in England the horn was still not firmly accepted as a solo instrument in its own right. Al's Hollywood Bowl performance did much to change this attitude. In fact he had already appeared in a solo capacity elsewhere—for example in Mozart's Fourth Horn Concerto with the Little Symphony Orchestra and Adolf Tandler—and was fast making a reputation as an expert chamber music player in appearances with the Los Angeles Music Society.

A significant feature of Al's character was his forceful and outspoken nature and his championing of those colleagues whom he considered had been ill treated. He was always helping those less talented than himself and protecting their positions. There were many occasions when he threatened to resign if a player's position were jeopardized by unfair practice. His organizing ability received an outlet in 1934 when William Andrews Clark, the manager of the Hollywood Bowl, died. The remainder of the committee was paralysed by the loss of the man on whom they had come to rely so much. The members of the orchestra therefore stepped in, headed by Al as manager, and saved the Bowl from financial disaster by running the remainder of the season's concerts themselves, with considerable success.

For the moment, however, Al's horn-playing eclipsed his managerial abilities. For many seasons now the Philharmonic's principal conductor had been Artur Rodzinski and he was quick to appreciate the standard of Al's musicianship and the high reputation it had earned. Of one performance Rodzinski conducted, Tchaikovsky's Fifth Symphony, one paper said:

Alfred Brain, first horn-player, and Vladmir Drucker, trumpeter, gave to the melodies for brass such distinction and beauty of tone as to emphasise anew the fact that our orchestra can boast of this section and the woodwinds in any orchestral company in the world.

When Rodzinski moved to Cleveland in 1934 he persuaded Al to go with him and for two seasons, from 1934 to 1936, Al was first horn of the Cleveland Orchestra. There, too, he was able to pursue his chamber-music interests in the Cleveland Woodwind Ensemble, bringing such works as Ibert's *Three Short Pieces* before the Cleveland public for the first time.

Al returned to Los Angeles in 1936 and took stock of his current position. He was now fifty and wisely anticipated retirement from full-time playing. He needed a new interest which would also provide a source of income, so that he could ease himself out gently. For one season, however, he postponed the decision, playing again as first horn in the Philharmonic. The following spring the chance came to purchase some property and he and Straussie moved to Palms Station, not far outside Los Angeles, where they set to work to build up a chicken farm.

Al did not lose touch with the musical world, however. He continued to play for the film studios, and then on 7 May 1939 was invited back to the Philharmonic to lead the horns for the orchestra's first broadcast on Columbia Radio. The conductor for that concert was the orchestra's new musical director, a Dr Otto Klemperer who was living and working in California as a refugee from Nazi Germany. Al also became involved in musical politics at this time, being elected local representative of the area MTA (the

American equivalent of the British Musicians' Union) in December 1940.

The war years did not wreak the same havoc on the American musical world as on the British, but there was inevitably some recession. Al's 'retirement' from full-time playing had thus been timely. He spent the war years putting the chicken farm on a firm commercial basis with such success that he opened a shop; 'Brain's Poultry Store', open on Fridays and Saturdays, sold fresh chickens raised on Al and Straussie's own farm. By 1944, when his nephew Dennis visited him on an RAF band tour, the day's takings from the farm amounted to over a hundred dollars. Al had played one more season for the Los Angeles Philharmonic from 1943–4 and then took out a permanent contract as first horn for Twentieth-Century Fox. Film work enabled him to do as much horn-playing as he wanted and still have time to run the farm.

Al played principal horn for Twentieth-Century Fox for nearly ten years; his second horn was Lawrence Sansone Jr, son of the New York horn manufacturer. Al's playing can still be heard on countless early post-war classics of the screen, and here, too, he was able to transmit something of his personality through the quality of his playing. For one film he played a difficult solo with exemplary skill and when members of the orchestra turned to voice their approval he calmly retorted: 'What's the matter? Haven't you heard a horn solo before?"

During the late 1940s Al returned to orchestral playing, this time for the Janssen Symphony Orchestra. Werner Janssen was an excellent composer and arranger; he had worked for Paramount Films and had written the score for *The General Died at Dawn*. His orchestra was made up largely from players in the Los Angeles Philharmonic and combined a modest number of concerts with some recordings for Capitol; it also broadcast for the Westinghouse Electric Company. Of the recordings, three featured Al as a soloist. Probably the best was that of Villa-Lobos's Choros no. 4 for three horns and trombone; he also played in an arrangement of "The Rosary", a then well known song by Ethelbert Nevin, which was a tribute to Al on leaving the Janssen Orchestra, but the recording did not display his playing at its best. Nor did the third record, of Haydn's Concerto no. 2 in D; Al showed many of the fine qualities that distinguished his pre-war playing—nobility of tone, ease of execution and confident attack—but he was over sixty and age had aggravated his weaknesses. His difficulty in obtaining the lowest notes made the Haydn concerto, with its frequent leaps to and from pedal notes, a particularly unfortunate choice. For the recording these were 'dubbed in' for him by a colleague but (for these were the early days of long-playing records) without sufficient technical skill to disguise the fact.

Al finally retired from horn-playing in 1954, at the age of sixty-nine, but certainly not from active life. He was a founder member of the Horn Club of Los Angeles and on 5 January 1952 had been host to its inaugural meeting. On retirement Al and Straussie sold their chicken farm and moved to Chatsworth, in the San Fernando valley, where they had a new home built. There, for a while, they continued in business with a dry goods variety store; Al had become involved in Rotary Club work and many donations were made from the store's profits both to the Rotary Club and to the local parent-teachers' association.

The Chatsworth Rotary Club was comparatively new and Al had been a founder member and Director of International Service. When, in 1958, he was elected President, he and Straussie purchased and ran the 'Horn Inn', a restaurant where members could meet for lunch. The same year marked the first Chatsworth Fiesta and Parade, to celebrate the community's seventy-second anniversary, and under the active guidance of Al and his committee it was organized and sponsored by the Rotary Club. For his services to the Club he was later elected an honorary member. The Rotary Club did not represent Al's sole interest in the community. His concern for young people led him to organize the Chatsworth Youth Foundation, and Christmas baskets from the store found their way there, in addition to the parent-teachers' association. In 1960 he was made a life-member of the PTA in recognition of his youth work.

Suddenly, on 29 March 1966, at the age of eighty, Al died after a heart attack. Although he had not been active in the Los Angeles musical world for over twenty years, and in the film world for over ten, many of his old friends, colleagues and admirers came to the funeral at the Little Church of The Flowers in Forest Lawn. Arrangements of Palestrina's *Stabat Mater* and the Funeral March from *Götterdämmerung* were played by hornists James Decker,

Leon Donfrey, Sinclair Lott, George Hyde, Arthur Briegleb, John Cave and Alan and Gale Robinson. Tributes came from all over the USA and abroad; few men had earned such wide affection and admiration both as musician and servant of his fellow men. Perhaps this, from the MTA *Journal*, is his most fitting epitaph:

A gentleman he was, in every connotation of the word. Pleasant and gracious to everyone with whom he came in contact in any way, he had a tremendous zest for living. A gracious host and an excellent chef, his parties are among my finest memories. A raconteur—lover of Gilbert and Sullivan, and of limericks which he could recite by the hour—his eyes sparkled with a twinkle which lighted up every gathering at which he was present.

To say only that Alf held a position of dominance as the almost universally acknowledged greatest horn-player in the world is to understate the immense respect the man so justly earned.

Alfred Brain will be sorely missed—by me, personally, and by all musicians everywhere. To have known him was a privilege and an honor. And probably as fitting a farewell to him as words can express may be found in Shakespeare, whose writing Alf so dearly loved: 'Good-night, sweet prince'.

❧ 3 ❧

Father Aubrey

When Alfred emigrated to the United States in the autumn of 1922 he left the way open at last for his brother Aubrey to take over as London's leading horn-player. By November Aubrey had been appointed first horn of the Royal Philharmonic Society (with his father as second horn) and first horn of the Queen's Hall Orchestra. He still led the horns in the New Symphony and was soon to join Covent Garden as their first horn. Only the London Symphony remained, but this was to elude his grasp for another year yet. Thomes Busby shared the first horn desk with Van der Meerschen and it was November 1923 before Aubrey was able to return to the LSO, and only then as co-principal with Busby.

On 15 April 1923 Adolf Borsdorf died. He had played very little in public since before the war but his passing was keenly felt in the musical world as the loss of a man who had done perhaps more than any other to raise the standards of horn-teaching in England. It is worth remembering that as well as Alfred and Aubrey Brain he could number among his pupils such fine players as his sons, Oskar, Francis and Emil, and Frank Probyn. The example set by his playing also inspired countless others of lesser talent.

Borsdorf's death left vacant the professorships at both the Royal Academy and Royal College of Music. Aubrey naturally coveted both and with the help of his father devoted his energies to obtaining the post at the Royal Academy. The Royal College he took for granted; he was, after all, an ex-pupil and Borsdorf himself was a good precedent for holding both jobs. But Aubrey made a sad miscalculation. He indeed had little difficulty in winning the Royal Academy appointment, but to his surprise, and annoyance, the Royal College gave their post to Frank

Probyn. It was a bitter blow and a disappointment Aubrey found hard to forget.

One of his first pupils at the Academy was his own brother Arthur. A tall, charming man, 'Eddie', as he was affectionately known, was born in 1901 and studied at the Academy from September 1919, when he won an orchestral scholarship, until December 1923, soon after Aubrey's appointment. He was very promising and won both bronze and silver medals for horn-playing at the Academy, but soon after graduating he seemed to lose heart. If Aubrey had found it difficult to make any headway in the profession, Eddie found it well-nigh impossible. As he admitted, it was just no use trying to compete, and within a year or two he joined the City of London Police.

That same summer of 1923 Aubrey made his Prom début with Mozart's Second Horn Concerto and laid the foundations of his career as a soloist. As his father wrote to Alfred later, it was a great success and "got a nice notice in *The Times*". His position now firmly established in London's musical life, Aubrey spent the next few years widening his experience. Covent Garden was particularly attractive; the British National Opera Company had run five seasons from May 1922 to February 1924, and then the Grand Opera Syndicate had taken over. Aubrey was able to play in every kind of production with a succession of notable conductors, beginning with Bruno Walter's *Ring*. In 1927 the London Symphony Orchestra became the official 'pit' orchestra at Covent Garden. By then Aubrey had been principal horn for four years, for on 4 April 1924 Thomas Busby had resigned from the LSO after a disagreement with the board, leaving his posts of managing director, permanent director and secretary, as well as his position as co-principal horn with Aubrey. From then onwards the LSO elected all its officers. As principal horn, Aubrey took part not only in concerts and the opera but also in the growing number of fine recordings being made. With its principal conductor, Albert Coates, the LSO made many excellent records for HMV's black label—*Till Eulenspiegel*, Siegfried's Rhine Journey and the Prelude to *Rheingold* among them. Elgar also recorded nearly all his most important compositions with them.

These early records helped to spread Aubrey's reputation as an orchestral player. Even today it is possible to catch something from them of the ethereal quality of his tone and his stylish grace of phrasing. He could also be heard on Columbia's records as first horn of the Queen's Hall Orchestra and with his father on Edison Bell. The latter company had their own orchestra with the rather grandiose title of 'Royal Symphony Orchestra', which was conducted for many recordings by Joe Batten, the recording manager. Edison Bell's green label records appeared regularly over a period of eight years, from 1920 to 1927. Not long before they went into liquidation in the latter year, Aubrey had the distinction of making with them the first-ever recording of a horn concerto— Mozart's Second Concerto K 417 which he had played at the Proms again the previous September with Henry Wood. The recording, conducted as usual by Joe Batten, was tackled in a most peculiar manner. The first movement was cut fairly drastically, presumably to avoid splitting it between two sides of a disc, and the work thus fitted exactly onto three sides, one movement per side. This left a fourth side and rather than leave it blank Aubrey recorded Glazunov's *Reverie* for horn and piano; his accompanist was his wife Marion.

As Aubrey later commented, the records helped enormously to bring the horn before the public as a solo instrument in its own right. He wrote:

I believe the public would appreciate hearing more but there is so little music to choose from. I hope musicians will devote more of their attention to compositions of this nature so as to bring it into greater prominence. I do not think composers know enough of the French Horn to write for it and they apparently will not take the trouble to learn its complications. For it is a most complicated and difficult instrument, both to play and write for. I play solos whenever I can, but the opportunities are too few.

One such composer who took up the challenge was Ethel Smyth, who wrote a Concerto in A for violin and horn. At a Henry Wood concert on 5 March 1927 she conducted its first performance, Jelly d'Aranyi and Aubrey as the soloists. The new work was particularly suited to Aubrey's technique. It contained many wide leaps for the horn-player which he could manage with little difficulty. His embouchure was almost that of a trumpeter, his lower lip well within the rim of the mouthpiece; this gave him great facility over the lower two thirds of the horn's compass, without having to change his lip position significantly. The concerto also contains chords for the horn in the cadenza to the last movement. This acoustic phenomenon, previously used by Weber in his Concertino for horn written over one hundred years previously, is achieved by the player humming one note and at the same time playing another a suitable interval apart; three- or four-note chords arise from the reinforcement of certain overtones which are always present when two notes are sounded together. Aubrey repeated the concerto at the Proms later in 1927 with Antonio Brosa (violin); Ethel Smyth again conducted and, always the eccentric, annoyed the critics by not only making a short speech about the concerto but even turning round to signal to the audience as Aubrey was about to play the chords! The concerto had a mixed reception from the press. Francis Toye in the *Morning Post* complained that the horn merged too much in tone with that of the orchestra while the *Daily Telegraph* thought it Ethel Smyth's most attractive work to date. *Musical Opinion* wrote: 'Jelly d'Aranyi was joined by Aubrey Brain who played with his well-known distinction. The players received a cordial ovation.' The *Musical Times* (April 1927) is worth quoting in full, particularly for its comments on the chords:

. . . first performance of a fresh and vital new work by Dame Ethel Smyth, a concerto in A for violin, horn and orchestra in three movements. The themes were simple and always to the point although the form seemed loose and patchy. The soloists (Jelly d'Aranyi and Aubrey Brain) did ample justice to the work, the latter having difficult nuts to crack in the last movement—one wonders if musically they were worth cracking—where the horn has to produce a succession of pianissimo chords and low notes, which is seldom heard in the concert-hall.

One person who *was* intrigued by the chords was Bruno Walter. He was determined that the new work should be heard in Berlin at the earliest opportunity. On 19 December 1928, in a concert of Ethel Smyth's works in which she shared the conducting of the Berlin Philharmonic Orchestra with Walter, Aubrey was joined in Berlin by violinist Marjorie Hayward and thus became the first English horn-player to perform a solo concerto abroad—a rare distinction.

During 1927 Aubrey made no less than six broadcasts in both

solo and chamber works. Among them was the Brahms op. 40 Trio with Arthur Catterall (violin) and John Wills (piano) and two performances of the Schubert Octet with members of the 'Covent Garden Octet'. Aubrey also took part in three Mozart concerto performances, the last a relay from the Proms on 16 August; both the earlier performances were with the 'Wireless Symphony Orchestra', conducted by Edward Clark, and marked Aubrey's first association with one of the most important developments in the London orchestral world.

During the 1920s English orchestral standards had declined markedly, a decline which was highlighted by the visit of the Berlin Philharmonic Orchestra with Furtwängler in December 1927. At once there was an outcry: how could the excellence of this superb orchestra be matched? The answer came from the BBC, which had already made experiments in presenting orchestral music. When broadcasting first began in 1922, a Wireless Orchestra of nine players was formed and for a while this sufficed. During the early months of 1924 the BBC staged a series of six concerts in Central Hall, Westminster, using the Royal Albert Hall, London Symphony or Royal Philharmonic Orchestras. For the following winter they formed a permanent 'Wireless Symphony Orchestra' of thirty-seven players, which could be augmented to between sixty and seventy. With the Birmingham Symphony Orchestra four concerts were given at Covent Garden. In 1926 and 1927 the Wireless Symphony Orchestra and the Covent Garden Orchestra itself were combined for twelve National Concerts in the Royal Albert Hall.

After the Berlin Philharmonic's visit, Sir Thomas Beecham was the first to lay before them plans for a permanent, high-quality symphony orchestra. His scheme, however, was not suited to the demands of broadcasting. The BBC went on with plans of its own for a full-scale symphony orchestra which could be broken down into smaller units for broadcasting purposes, without overworking the players. A provisional symphony orchestra was formed and during the winter of 1929–30 gave a trial season of twenty-two symphony concerts, some of them part of Beecham's 1929 Delius Festival. Then in June 1930 it was put on a firm contractual basis and the BBC Symphony Orchestra was born.

Aubrey had joined the Wireless Symphony Orchestra when

Percy Pitt first conducted it in 1927; the horn quartet was then Aubrey, Harold Hamilton, Frank Probyn and H. F. Thornton. He still played regularly as first horn for all the other principal London orchestras but gradually, as the BBC made increasing demands on his time, relinquished them one by one. The declining fortunes and standards of these orchestras made the break easier. His last appearance with the London Symphony Orchestra was on 8 April 1929, after which he was replaced by Aubrey Thonger, who had been co-principal with him since November 1928. The Queen's Hall Orchestra was an ageing institution; the BBC took over the Proms in the summer of 1929 and the orchestra made its last public appearance at the 1930 Norwich Festival. After that it only reappeared on an *ad hoc* basis for gramophone recordings—such as the "Song of the Rhine Daughters", an arrangement of excerpts from *Götterdämmerung* made by Henry Wood which features Aubrey in some excellent horn-playing. Aubrey remained longest with the Royal Philharmonic Society; the last occasion on which he played first horn with them was on 13 March 1930.

Before he finally committed himself to the BBC Symphony Orchestra, Aubrey took part in a memorable recording, made on 8 May 1929, of the 'Abscheulicher' recitative and aria from Beethoven's *Fidelio*, which contains obbligato parts for three horns of exceptional difficulty. The soprano soloist was the great Frieda Leider and the orchestra was conducted by John Barbirolli. After a perfect 'take' in Kingsway Hall the orchestra was on the point of packing up when a very agitated Fred Gaisberg, the recording manager, telephoned to say that the recording line had not been connected! (The recording was being transmitted by land line to a studio off Leicester Square.) After desperate attempts to find another vacant hall, one was eventually located and the entire company transported there by taxi. That the recording was eventually so good is miracle enough; but the upheaval seemed to have had no effect on Aubrey or the other horn-players, who all performed brilliantly.

On 25 October 1929 Aubrey's father, A. E. Brain (senior) died, after only three years of retirement. The death of Letitia in 1923 had taken its toll physically as well as mentally. There were recurrent bouts of his old chest trouble, and in 1926 his doctor diagnosed bronchial asthma and emphysema of the lungs, declaring him totally unfit to work. He applied for assistance to the Royal Society of Musicians and left the Queen's Hall and Covent Garden Orchestras. He married again and spent his three remaining years as comfortably as his health would allow. Now 'Papa' Brain was gone. Bluff, kindly and utterly reliable, he had laid the foundations of a tradition of English horn-playing which was already flourishing. He had lived to see two of his sons become the leading players of their day; when he died his loss was also mourned by his eight-year-old grandson, Dennis, who was destined to become the greatest of them all.

With Aubrey Brain as first horn the new BBC Symphony Orchestra made its first public appearance at the 1930 Promenade season, conducted by Henry Wood. Its true début, however, with its newly appointed conductor, Dr Adrian Boult, was on 22 October of that year. The concert was a stunning success; the programme—Wagner's overture to *The Flying Dutchman*, Saint-Saëns's Cello Concerto (with Suggia), Brahms's Fourth Symphony and Ravel's Second *Daphnis and Chloë* Suite—showed that its players could cope with the most demanding works. Nearly half the players, like Aubrey, came from the London Symphony Orchestra, and all who heard that first concert agreed that here was enormous potential and a sufficient reply to Ernest Newman's criticism in the *New York Times*, written after the visit to London of the New York Philharmonic with Toscanini in 1930, that English orchestral playing was 'atrocious'. The BBC themselves were so pleased and confident at the success of their new orchestra that Richard Strauss, Felix Weingartner and Bruno Walter were invited to come and conduct it during its second season.

The BBC Symphony Orchestra virtually monopolized London's music. Its contracts, issued in June 1930, demanded one hundred per cent loyalty from its players. They were well paid and there was little time for outside engagements. The new orchestra had sounded the death-knell for the Royal Albert Hall Orchestra and was soon to do the same for the Royal Philharmonic. Only the London Symphony Orchestra survived, chaired by the one surviving member of 'God's Own Quartet'—Henri Van der Meerschen, but even he was soon no more. In very poor health, he retired from the orchestra in October 1932 and died just six months later.

With only the BBC Symphony and the London Symphony

Orchestras as the largest employers of musicians there still remained a large reserve of good players who welcomed regular orchestral work. There was also one conductor, Sir Thomas Beecham, who had little cause to be sympathetic towards the BBC. When he offered his ideas and services to the London Symphony Orchestra and was promptly snubbed by them, he retaliated by forming his own new orchestra, the London Philharmonic, which made its first appearance on 7 October 1932. Here was the opening for the many players not attached either to the BBC or the London Symphony, though it is interesting to note that over one quarter of Beecham's players came from the latter organization. Principal horn at the outset was Francis Bradley (the son of Adolf Borsdorf), but he left after one season to join the BBC, and Charles Gregory became permanent first horn.

Beecham's treatment of his horn section in the LPO is both interesting and relevant. Some interest had been shown in the 1920s in the wide-bore German horns—'cows' horns' as Thomas Busby disparagingly dubbed them—particularly after the 1927 visit by the Berlin Philharmonic Orchestra. In the LPO Beecham insisted that the whole horn section should be equipped with German horns and paid for them. Aubrey, by contrast, was adamant that not only he but the entire BBC horn section should retain the narrow-bore French instrument, an eccentricity based on a reasoned philosophy. Writing in *Monthly Musical Record* in July 1931 he maintained that "the most casual of listeners, hearing a performance by a German orchestra, cannot but be struck by the peculiar euphonium-like quality of the horn tone". Aubrey realized that he and his colleagues were in a minority; the continental players did have greater volume of sound, and the rotary valves gave greater ease of execution, but for sheer *purity* of sound the Raoux horn was unsurpassable. Those who heard Aubrey 'in the flesh' agree, and even records of the time bear some testimony to his argument. But he neglected one important factor. Business interests demanded that players of lesser calibre adopt the large-bore horn to safeguard their very livelihood. They dared not risk 'cracking' notes with the narrow-bore instrument, when players such as Aubrey had demonstrated that the element of uncertainty was inherent not in the instrument but the player. Besides, Aubrey had achieved his own fabulous suc-

D

cess despite, rather than because of, the narrow-bore French horn;
he carried on a tradition set by his masters—Borsdorf, Paersch and
his own father—all of whom were mature artists when the wide-
bore horn first appeared on the market and therefore unwilling to
learn the new techniques involved. Eccentric he may have been,
but he was a constant reminder that reliability and tone quality
are not as incompatible as many might imagine. He did admit
that continental players were sensible enough to have uniformity
of instruments within each horn section, hence his own insistence
in the BBC that *all* the players should use French horns 'to ensure
equality and balance of tone'.

Beecham's own policy proved useful to Aubrey. When, in 1933,
the London Philharmonic replaced the London Symphony as the
'pit' orchestra at Covent Garden, a number of brand-new Raoux
horns were found under the stage. They were no use to the LPO
so they were sold; Aubrey bought two of them—one for himself
and one as a spare, possibly for either of his two sons should they
want to take the instrument up. He found a use for one of them
sooner than he imagined when he succeeded in backing his car
over his original instrument, completely flattening the crook.

In 1933 Serge Koussevitsky came to London to share with Boult
the conducting of the London Music Festival. At one rehearsal he
had occasion to reprimand Aubrey for playing too quietly for his
second to maintain both balance and audibility. "Mr Brain, do not
be so silly and play so quietly that your second cannot be heard."
This insensitivity to others was an attribute which perhaps eman-
ated from Aubrey's rather shallow character. His conversation,
in fact almost his whole life, was confined to horns and horn-
playing; his one outside interest was in cars, which he repaired
himself, being a very practical man. Never one to go for a drink
'with the lads' after a concert, his somewhat sedate nature earned
him the nickname of 'Custard'. Superficially he was a very charming man; his good looks made him the idol of the girls at the
Royal Academy and for a number of years he carried on an affair
with Muriel Hart, the viola player. The affair had no sexual
overtones, but it made Aubrey the object of some ridicule and a
rather lonely man, often accused of conceit, perhaps wrongly.

In no doubt, however, was Aubrey's skill as a horn-player, indeed as a musician. He had perfect pitch and his almost infallible

accuracy of attack was attributed by many to his habit of humming quietly the note he was about to play. While we have seen that he may have demonstrated some lack of consideration as an orchestral player his skill and discretion in chamber-music was of an outstanding order. Since 1927 he had been a regular broadcaster in chamber works and gave frequent public recitals, despite the restrictions of BBC life. A typical performance was in 1934 at the Wigmore Hall with Adolf Busch and Rudolf Serkin. After violin sonatas by Mozart and Beethoven, Busch and Serkin were joined by Aubrey for the Brahms Trio op. 40. One press tribute noted:

> Everything was beyond question in Brahms' trio. A performance that underrates Brahms is unbearable but Mr Busch and his friends declared themselves the most fervent believers. Mr Brain's horn part had never a flaw, and the delicacy with which his instrument entered into the ensemble was wonderful. That memory must be a long one which can recall a finer performance of Brahms' op. 40.

Shortly afterwards the same three artists recorded the Trio for HMV, a set that remained in the catalogues for nearly twenty years until the demise of 78 rpm records. It returned, transferred to long-playing discs, and was available until very recently, appropriately on the label "Great Recordings of the Century". Great it certainly was and for years the yardstick by which subsequent recordings were always judged.

Another work recorded by Aubrey which also reappeared on the same label was Bach's Brandenburg Concerto no. 1, made in 1935 as part of a set of the complete Brandenburg Concertos by Adolf Busch and his chamber players. It was the year of the BBC Symphony Orchestra's first foreign trip—to Brussels on 12 March for a concert in the Palais des Beaux Arts. Francis Bradley had joined the BBC as second horn for the 1934–5 season, leaving the London Philharmonic after two years as their principal horn. He joined Aubrey in the Brandenburg recording which was made in only one session, on a Sunday morning. Both players used B♭ crooks; this was an unusual departure as only four years before Aubrey had written: "A more questionable advantage [of the German horn] is the horn in B♭. No doubt it facilitates the execution of high or difficult passages; but here tone and intonation are sacrificed to such an extent as utterly to destroy the characteristics of the instrument." In the Brandenburg the very high tessitura of the horn parts undoubtedly demands the use of a small crook, whatever the sacrifice in tone quality. Purist though Aubrey was, he was too wily to take unnecessary risks and never hesitated to take to any fingering or crook that made the notes more secure. He also used the B♭ crook on his recording of Borodin's *Prince Igor* overture.

It is regrettable that more solo horn works were not recorded during these years. The Smyth concerto, for example, had been twice performed at the Proms (in 1927 and 1932) and twice broadcast, but no recording had been attempted. It must be remembered, however, that Aubrey's 1927 recording of the Mozart K 417 Concerto had been the first horn concerto *ever* recorded. Ten years later, the public was at last beginning to accept the horn as a respectable solo instrument but not yet on a scale sufficient to merit recordings of works that possessed only limited appeal. The Bach Brandenburg and the Brahms Trio were not horn concertos and attracted the record-buying public for more than the quality of their horn-playing, outstanding though it undoubtedly was.

Aubrey's other recordings likewise did not feature him as a soloist, although in December 1926 he played a short extract on a record illustrating the instruments of the orchestra. During the same year he recorded the Brahms Trio for the National Gramophone Society with Spencer Dyke and York Bowen; poor balancing makes the horn sometimes almost inaudible. A better recording made by the Society two years later with the added advantages brought by electrical recording, is of the Mozart Piano and Wind Quintet, with Kathleen Long as the pianist. Then for Columbia Aubrey recorded the Beethoven Septet and the Schubert Octet, both with members of the Lener Quartet. The only other disc which specifically mentions Aubrey's name in the 1930s was DA 1318, a ten-inch recording made by Boult and the BBC Symphony Orchestra of the Nocturne from Mendelssohn's *Midsummer Night's Dream*.

The pianist Harriet Cohen, who took part in the first performance of Arnold Bax's Octet for solo horn, piano and strings at the Aeolian Hall on 11 December 1936, has recalled Aubrey's qualities as a chamber-music player. "That divine horn-player . . . something so beautiful about his tone that would have ravished Debussy, that I feel compelled to say that he was one of the very greatest artists with whom I ever performed." Another composer who admired Aubrey's talents was York Bowen; he had studied the horn as a young man and had also taken part in many recitals as Aubrey's accompanist or partner in chamber works. In 1938 he wrote a Horn Sonata which he dedicated to Aubrey, and together they gave the first performance in the same year.

During the 1930s the BBC Symphony Orchestra had become one of the most competent and versatile orchestras in Europe; its reputation was such that the world's leading conductors were happy to be associated with it. One was Toscanini, who first conducted the orchestra in June 1935; he had previously been in Britain in 1930 at the end of a European tour with the Philharmonic Symphony Orchestra of New York. For the four Queen's Hall concerts in June 1935 he cut short many of the rehearsals, such was his delight with the orchestra. In 1936 came the BBC Symphony's first European tour—to Paris, Zurich, Vienna and Budapest—and then Toscanini returned for four more visits between 1937 and 1939. Three of these visits (October 1937, June 1938 and May 1939) included recording sessions, and some of the performances are still in the catalogues. Many other notable conductors made memorable recordings with the BBC; some which featured Aubrey especially include Fritz Busch with *Till Eulenspiegel*, Boult with the overtures to *Der Freischütz* and *Hansel and Gretel*, Walter with Mozart's Symphony no. 39 and Brahms's Symphony no. 4 as well as Elgar with some of his own compositions.

Aubrey's contribution to both public and recorded orchestral performances was outstanding. His attack was supremely confident and the purity of his tone thrilled the listener in much the same way as that of his brother Alfred. But Aubrey achieved this magic in a very different way; he had started to learn the horn at an earlier age and so used less pressure than either Alf or their teacher, Borsdorf. His embouchure, mentioned above in connection with the Smyth concerto, was well suited to the lower two thirds of the horn's compass. That great exponent of horn technique, W. H. Blandford, described Aubrey as basically a low-register player with a 'high break', that is, he had to adjust his lips for the highest notes; this was in contrast with Alfred (and, later, Dennis) who had greater ease in the higher register and a 'low break' to reach the lower notes. Above all, Aubrey's tone had a classical purity which kept alive all that was best in the traditions of English horn-playing, and as a fine teacher he instilled this into countless pupils.

On the night after Sir Henry Wood's Jubilee Concert at the Royal Albert Hall, which had marked his fifty years of conducting and in which Rachmaninov played his own Second Piano Concerto before an enormous audience, Aubrey brought before the public one of his pupils who was to carry on those traditions he held so dear. Adolf Busch was presenting another of his 'series' concerts; on this occasion, 6 October 1938, the programme was all Bach—the Brandenburg Concertos nos. 1, 3 and 5.

As the orchestra assembled in the Queen's Hall, the audience had little difficulty in recognizing Aubrey in his usual seat as first horn; but next to him was a seventeen-year-old boy making his public début—Aubrey's own son, Dennis.

◦§ 4 §◦

Schooldays and
Royal Academy

Dennis was Aubrey Brain's second son. Born in London on 17 May 1921, he was his brother Leonard's junior by six years. In such a musical family it was natural to suppose that Dennis would become a musician, but even with a father, two uncles, and a grandfather all horn-players it was not inevitable that he too would take up the horn. His brother Leonard in fact began a career in chemistry and when he gave this up to join the music profession it was as a very accomplished oboist. Dennis, however, heard his father practise at home and showed an interest in the horn from an early age. Leonard remembers that Dennis was only three when he saw his father practising one day and asked to be allowed to try. The horn was put to his lips and after a few attempts a perfect note emerged. Such precociousness was not exploited by his parents. Aubrey believed that pupils should start the horn only when their teeth and embouchure were fully developed, in their teens. He did, however, let Dennis blow the horn every Saturday morning as a treat.

Marion was anxious that both her boys should have as good an education as possible and consequently Dennis was sent, at the age of seven, to Richmond Hill Preparatory School. It was close to their home and Dennis travelled to and fro each day by 'bus. Soon afterwards he began piano lessons. His mother was herself an excellent player but was wise enough not to teach her own son; she sent him to a very good local teacher with whom he made rapid progress. He did get an introduction to brass instruments as well, playing the bugle in the school cadet band.

When he was nine Dennis developed glandular fever and in

November 1930 had an operation to remove his tonsils and adenoids. During the operation the surgeon accidentally severed the olfactory nerve, leaving Dennis with no sense of smell—and, as a result, very little taste—for the rest of his life. He spent four months convalescing at the Yarrow Home in Broadstairs, a resort with which he was familiar since Aubrey took the whole family there each summer for the holidays.

From prep. school Dennis followed Leonard to St Paul's School, Kensington, where he joined the Modern side. Here was a great wealth of musical activity. He joined the school choir and became a keen and valuable member, though he was not a solo treble. There were also record programmes and regular concerts. At these Dennis often played piano solos; on one occasion he played Mendelssohn's Rondo Capriccioso in E and for the 1935 Christmas concert the first movement of Beethoven's G major Sonata op. 49 no. 2. Dennis had said nothing at home about the Beethoven performance. He practised secretly at school and on the night surprised his family by walking on to the stage and playing like a seasoned professional. Several in the audience that evening noticed in his playing the same cool precision and musicianship that were later to distinguish his horn-playing.

Dennis continued his piano lessons with the school's Director of Music, Henry Wilson. Wilson, who was also on the staff of the Royal College of Music, encouraged him to take up the organ. The school possessed two instruments and there were five or six other pupils learning at the time, among them Peter Racine Fricker (later a composer and now professor at the University of California) whom Dennis also met in a small class for higher mathematics. Despite occasional rows over whose turn it was to practise, Dennis and Peter became close friends. Dennis was able later to help to promote some of his friend's music and was in turn rewarded with new outlets for his own talents.

Dennis also joined the school scout troop which he supported with enthusiasm and interest but, like sport, without any special devotion. One master who taught him remembers that the outstanding qualities he showed at school were integrity, friendly cheerfulness, an entirely natural boyishness, robust temperament and lively responsiveness to all that was best in school life. In brief, he was entirely normal; nothing in his behaviour could have been further from the popular notion of the budding young genius.

In the summer of 1936, after only three years at St Paul's, Dennis persuaded his father to take him away from school and allow him to go to the Royal Academy of Music.

"After all," he told Leonard, "I'm not likely to get my School Certificate so I might as well go to the Academy." There was a more compelling incentive. Only months before, Aubrey had quite casually said:

"I've found another instrument; would you like to see what you can do with it?" It was another Raoux, the twin of Aubrey's own, which he had bought from Covent Garden in 1933. Again, no pressure was put upon Dennis, but he took to it at once and Aubrey gave him lessons at home. His progress must have been remarkable for him to consider the horn rather than the piano as his principal study at the Academy. Aubrey was professor there and indeed proposed his name for admission. This undoubtedly influenced Dennis's choice of college; but he was so anxious to gain admission on his own merit, and not because of his father's influence, however, that he entered for the W. Stokes special scholarship grant and won it. This entitled him to free tuition for one year. He joined the Academy in September 1936, to study the horn with his father, the piano with Max Pirani, harmony with Montague Phillips, as well as conducting and aural training.

Every morning Dennis received three quarters of an hour's tuition on the horn from his father. This was probably more than most students were lucky enough to get, but the system was sufficiently fluid to accommodate such a special arrangement. Aubrey also sensed that his son was more than usually gifted but he was anxious not to push him any faster than his abilities would permit. Nor did he allow Dennis to 'have a go' at anything; practice and adequate preparation were all-important. For the time being the Academy orchestras and the London Senior Orchestra were considered sufficient for Dennis to cope with. Sir Henry Wood frequently conducted the Academy's First Orchestra in both rehearsals and concerts, not only in the Academy's own Duke's Hall but in the Queen's Hall as well. At these concerts Dennis usually led the horn section under the watchful eye of his father, who 'sat in', as many of the staff did on these occasions.

There was so much activity at the Academy that any pupil who showed promise was soon brought to the fore. Herbert Withers was in charge of chamber music, organizing and rehearsing concerts which included the standard repertoire but also featured students' own compositions. The Beethoven Septet was a popular work and movements from it were played at a number of concerts during the spring term of Dennis's first year. On 3 May 1937 Dennis played third horn next to William Grant and Douglas Moore and Gerald Gover (piano) in a performance of Moore's own Adagio in C minor for three horns and piano.

At the end of his first year at the Academy Dennis won bronze medals for piano, horn, conducting and aural training; his Stokes scholarship grant was also extended for a further year, to July 1938. He was joined in the autumn term of 1937 by his brother Leonard. Leonard had taken a first degree in science and had already completed half his thesis for a doctorate but was able to keep himself from music no longer. He played the oboe—Aubrey had tried, in vain, to interest him in the horn but his natural stubbornness made him reject this and turn to something quite different. It was probably as well that he did, for he was not endowed with the 'Brain' jaw. It also meant that he could reinforce his superiority as the elder brother by unfailingly pointing out, with some immunity, Dennis's shortcomings as a horn-player. Dennis, with his puckish sense of humour, would gently get his revenge. "We must listen to what Leonard says," he would tell his friends in an audible whisper. "He's very clever; he's a *Ph.D.* you know!"

The difference in the two brothers' characters was not unlike that between Aubrey and Alfred, in fact if anything more marked. Many were heard to wonder how two such sedate and serious people as Aubrey and his wife Marion had produced two sons with such strong, yet completely opposed, personalities. Despite their differences, and their brotherly quarrels both Dennis and Leonard shared a passion for music, never more so than when they could play together in ensembles. That first term together at the Academy they found many opportunities for chamber music. The Mozart and Beethoven Quintets for piano and wind were firm favourites; the pianist was invariably their friend and fellow-student, Denis Matthews. The clarinettist was usually Alwyn Kell, brother of the famous Reginald, and James Richens the bassoonist.

Every summer term the Academy staged an opera. The July 1938 production was *The Marriage of Figaro*; Dennis played first horn, with John Burden as second—a partnership that soon ripened into a close friendship. Some time later, John Burden got together a small orchestra, mainly from the Academy, and Dennis played a horn concerto and an organ concerto for him, in the same concert. Playing for the opera was both enjoyable and valuable experience. It marked the end of another successful year; Dennis won the E. F. James Prize, silver medals for piano, horn and aural training, and the bronze medal for harmony. Most important of all he won the Ross Scholarship for wind players; this entitled him to a minimum of two years' free tuition, with an extension to three. The adjudicator was P. S. G. O'Donnell, one of a family of musicians with whom Dennis and many of his colleagues were to have much closer contact before very long.

Dennis changed from piano to organ in September 1938. His teacher was G. D. Cunningham, who had taught Dennis's uncle Alfred the piano nearly forty years before. Dennis had great respect for Cunningham both as man and musician—indeed he was able to confide in him about personal as well as musical matters. Over the next two years Dennis learnt a great deal from Cunningham about style and musicianship generally: he always said that his father taught him how to play the horn while Cunningham taught him how to play music. For his part, Cunningham regretted that Dennis chose the horn rather than the organ for his profession, since he believed Dennis could have had comparable success with either instrument.

The 1938 autumn term was an auspicious one for Dennis, for he made his public début on 6 October. His father had been asked by Adolf Busch, who was to conduct a Bach series at the Queen's Hall, to find a second horn for the Brandenburg Concerto no. 1. His former second, Francis Bradley, no longer played in the BBC Symphony Orchestra and so Aubrey took a chance and suggested Dennis as a substitute. Dennis himself had only one worry; it was the time of the Munich crisis and he was desperately anxious that something might prevent the Bach concert from taking place. His one ambition since joining the Academy had been to 'sit next to Dad in the orchestra'. Happily, it went ahead as planned, and Dennis's début was witnessed by many of his friends, who sat on the platform seats behind the orchestra. The event also aroused comment from the press. The *Daily Telegraph* wrote:

> In the F major concerto Aubrey Brain was in his accustomed place as first horn but he had a new partner, his 17-year-old son, Dennis, whose first appearance this was—a Queen's Hall event of no little interest. The famous family keeps up its traditions in the representative of the new generation. Son seconded father with a smoothness and certainty worthy of his name.

The concert became a talking-point at the Academy. One of the flautist Gareth Morris's earliest recollections of his Academy days is of someone proudly pointing out Dennis to him in the canteen. "That's Dennis Brain—he's only seventeen and has just played Bach Brandenburg no. 1 with his father in Queen's Hall." They met the following day at Henry Wood's First Orchestra rehearsal. The work under study was the Grieg Piano Concerto and Gareth was astonished to hear the horn echo his own solo in the first movement with precisely the same phrasing, so that there was complete continuity of musical thought. At the interval he made straight for Dennis and from that day they became firm friends; later, they discovered that their birthdays were only four days apart—Dennis's on 17 May and Gareth's on 13 May—which made an excuse for a special joint celebration, on the 15th. Gareth also joined the chamber music-making. He had already met Leonard and from his manner assumed him to be a lecturer, an illusion which soon vanished when he saw him sitting in the ranks of the First Orchestra!

The winter of 1938–9 was busy with many performances. Herbert Withers directed a series of five Mozart chamber music concerts; in addition to the K 452 Piano and Wind Quintet Dennis took part in the K 407 Quintet for horn and strings. This is a brilliant piece, almost a miniature concerto, and became a regular part of Dennis's ever-widening repertoire. Then, on 21 February 1939, the London Schubert Society presented a concert in the Academy's Duke's Hall. The programme consisted of the fourteen songs of *Schwanengesang* and the Octet for wind and strings. For the latter Dennis joined the Menges Quartet and Alwyn Kell, James Richens and Victor Watson. The *Daily Telegraph* commented:

The latter [the Octet], heard for the second time within eight days, again boasted a Kell as clarinet and a Brain as horn though they were not last week's players, the Kell being this time Alwyn (Reginald Kell's brother) and the horn not Aubrey the father but Dennis the son. . . . The poetic effect made by the horn . . . showed once again that the gift for wind-playing runs in families.

Two days after the Schubert concert, Dennis made his first gramophone recording. It was for Columbia; Walter Legge, their artists' manager, had engaged the Lener Quartet with Aubrey and Dennis to record the Mozart D major Divertimento K334 for two horns and strings. Dennis was already familiar with the work; earlier in the winter he had performed it with his father in Queen's Hall. Now, as then, he played second—the only recording ever made with Dennis as second horn, Walter Legge was most impressed on first meeting this young player. He had come across him 'warming up' in an empty studio, unable to believe the evidence of eye and ear, that this very young-looking seventeen-year-old was the masterly executant of the *Till Eulenspiegel* horn theme he had just interrupted. There is an amusing epilogue to this recording: one eminent gramophone journal noted that 'needless to say, what little the Brain *brothers* have to do, is scrupulously done'!

On 2 March Aubrey and Dennis broadcast the same Mozart Divertimento, this time with the Laurance Turner Quartet. By this time Dennis was no stranger to the BBC studios. A year previously he had taken part in a programme of Mozart horn duos with his father. After a shaky start he had settled down to play with cool precision and sense of style. A few weeks later he appeared as a soloist in a Monday evening magazine programme. The flautist, Gerald Jackson, was playing in the studio orchestra that evening and later recalled:

I cannot forget one early visitor. It was a boy brought along by Aubrey Brain, principal horn of the BBC Symphony Orchestra. He played a rondo from a Mozart horn concerto with staggering technique and style and provided our first encounter with the player whom Beecham called 'Siegfried' and whom we still mourn as Dennis Brain.

In December 1938 Dennis was one of the participants in a conductors' class concert arranged by Ernest Read. He already held

the bronze medal in conducting and now found an additional outlet for his interest. The spring and summer terms of 1939 were
particularly busy for Dennis. He joined his father yet again in the
Mozart D major Divertimento, this time on 25 April in Queen's
Hall as part of the London Music Festival. On 7 June there was
another in the series of concerts of students' compositions; this
one contained a Partita for wind quintet which Denis Matthews
had written for his friends at the Academy. It was performed by
David Sandeman (flute), Leonard and Dennis, with Margaret Jacob
(clarinet) and Mary Hunt (bassoon). The annual opera production
was Rutland Boughton's *The Immortal Hour*, and then came the
end of term with yet another impressive list of prizes. Dennis won
a silver medal for harmony, bronze medals in composition and
organ, and certificates in horn and aural training. All was now set
for Dennis's final year to be his most successful yet. The many
contacts he had already made and the experience he had gained,
made him hope for numerous professional openings when he
finally graduated. All these hopes were swept away on the outbreak of war in September 1939. Dennis's career was now to be
shaped by a wide variety of contrasting and unexpected developments.

Wartime Engagements

The onset of war in September 1939 interrupted Dennis's final year at the Academy and, for a while at least, the prospects of a career as a musician seemed very remote. Established players had their problems, too; all theatres and concert-halls were immediately closed, a panic measure because of expected air-raids. The BBC's Promenade season, nearly at its end and scheduled to include another performance of Ethel Smyth's Concerto with Aubrey Brain and Antonio Brosa, was suspended. On Sunday 3 September the whole BBC Symphony Orchestra was evacuated to new headquarters in Bristol. There, at least, it could continue to make music, albeit only to a limited degree for the time being. But for young men like Dennis 'call-up' was only a matter of time. In anticipation of this both Dennis and Leonard joined the RAF, enlisting on 26 September. Just one week too early to join for the duration of the war only, they had to sign on for the full term of seven years. After a period of basic training they were attached to the Central Band at Uxbridge and very soon became caught up in the new and exciting developments taking place there.

Squadron-Leader R. P. O'Donnell, conductor of the eighty-one strong RAF Central Band, had anticipated the problems of musicians in wartime. As soon as war broke out he proposed to the Air Ministry that a limited number of skilled musicians should be called up into the Central Band. Small units could then be made up for dispersal to camps both at home and abroad where they could provide entertainment and uplift.

"I want every camp to have its own music," O'Donnell appealed. "These camps will be isolated far from normal amusements. Music must always play a vital part in national life. I need at least a thousand professional musicians."

Air Ministry approval came quickly; so did the recruits. In response to a newspaper advertisement 980 musicians found their way to Uxbridge. Such a number was too unwieldy, and the inclusion of wind-players of the calibre of Dennis and Leonard Brain, Gareth Morris, Cecil James and Harold Jackson, along with string players such as Harry Blech, the Griller Quartet and many others, gave O'Donnell the idea of forming a symphony orchestra. Air Ministry approval was again sought; again it was given and by mid-1940 the RAF Symphony Orchestra had been born. There were thirty-two strings, led by Sergeant David Martin, and the wind-players were chosen from the Central Band.

Dennis was principal horn and from the outset was liked and respected by all the regular bandsmen who, after all, had cause enough to resent the influx of civilian professionals. Much of their respect for Dennis was a result of admiration for his playing. But life in the RAF Band was not exclusively musical. There were duties to be done—guard-duty, drill, polishing, scrubbing—all of which Dennis accepted and carried out with the minimum of fuss or complaint.

The RAF's second horn during the war was Norman Del Mar, a student from the Royal College of Music. His professor there, Frank Probyn, had arranged for him to have an audition for the RAF without telling him what he was applying for. Dennis and Norman became the greatest of friends and many years later Frank admitted that he had had a two-fold motive in engineering their meeting. He wanted Norman to learn as much as possible from Dennis about horn-playing, but he also believed that Dennis would in his turn benefit significantly from Norman's wider musical interests and sophistication. In the RAF they fast gained a reputation as the naughty boys in the corner, adapting the monotonous horn parts in a variety of subtle and amusing ways. The Air Force March became practically a horn concerto, while strange obbligato parts appeared in such well-known and wide-ranging favourites as Kreisler's *A King Stepped Out* and Rossini's overture *William Tell*. These pranks were the source of added amusement since O'Donnell rarely noticed them!

O'Donnell had pretensions but no real claims to be a conductor. He rarely used a baton and quickly acquired the nickname of 'Two-Gun Pete' from his habit of beating time with two pointed

DENNIS BRAIN'S
HORN-PLAYING
FOREBEARS
Grandfather A. E. Brain
(nearer camera) recording
for Edison Bell in 1925.
(*photo: Edison Bell*)

Father Aubrey when in
the BBC Symphony
Orchestra, 1936. (*photo:
BBC*)

Uncle Alfred during his
Queen's Hall days, about
1912. (*photo: courtesy
Sinclair Lott*)

Dennis's first horn during his last term at St. Paul's School, 1935. (*photo: courtesy Mrs J. Burden*)

Royal Academy 2 February 1939: a rehearsal of Grieg's *Der Einsame* with Richard Hargreaves (baritone), Dennis Brain and John Burden (horns); the strings are conducted by Herbert Withers. (*photo: courtesy Mrs. J. Burden*)

index fingers. Nevertheless, he and the RAF Orchestra provided an invaluable service to wartime Britain by taking concerts and re-citals of a high standard to all parts of the country (and later abroad). By far the greatest service, however, was to the musicians themselves, since they were able to pursue their own careers and interests provided that they could so arrange their engagements as not to interfere with their service duties.

In the very early days of the war the Royal Academy of Music found itself short of players and invited back those who could make themselves available. Both Dennis and Leonard returned to study for the spring and summer terms of 1940. The Academy not only paid their fares to and from Uxbridge but provided them with lunch as well! Aubrey was away with the BBC in Bristol and so Dennis continued only with his organ lessons, but at the end of the summer term he was awarded the John Solomon Prize for wind-players, his seventh award for horn-playing in his four years at the Academy.

During the summer of 1940 Dennis and Leonard began to look for rooms of their own in Uxbridge. There they did not have to live in camp—they had been in barracks at the start as their parents were in Bristol but envied the freedom of the many who lived out. In October 1940 they found a place of their own and number 16, The Greenway, became a regular meeting-place for their closest friends. It was also the scene, one memorable after-noon, of a remarkable horn lesson—one of the very few Dennis ever gave. As he and a group of friends were making their way back after lunch he apologetically asked to have the room to him-self for a while.

"I'm going to give a lesson," he grinned sheepishly.

Leonard, Gareth and the others obligingly waited downstairs and saw the pupil arrive. As they listened they could hear a succession of brilliant runs, scales, trills and arpeggios; then a brief silence and a moment later the sound of footsteps hurrying heavily down the back stairs and out of the building. They hurried up to Dennis's room.

"What results!" Gareth congratulated him, "and in such a short time."

Dennis grinned. "Well, actually it was me playing." He was still too inexperienced to take on the responsibility of teaching.

E

At that stage he simply knew how to play and genuinely believed that the only way to communicate this was by demonstration, to the astonishment and consternation of his pupil. In fact he did very little teaching throughout his career. On the whole there was not enough time except for just the occasional lesson. James Diack, who eventually became first horn of the BBC Welsh Symphony Orchestra, was one person who in later years had some regular lessons from Dennis.

The two Brain brothers shared that room in Uxbridge for three and a half years, a tribute to Dennis's easy-going nature and good-humoured tolerance of others. Leonard freely admitted that he was not the easiest of persons to live with, but throughout the entire period in Uxbridge he and Dennis had not a single quarrel. They also managed to agree to share Dennis's first car—a Morris 8 open two-seater—a very reliable vehicle which they used until the end of the war.

On 9 April 1940 Aubrey recorded Mozart's Third Horn Concerto with the BBC Symphony Orchestra and Sir Adrian Boult in the Colston Hall, Bristol. The first movement cadenza (written for him by his wife) is probably the best example of Aubrey's superb purity of tone. He took infinite pains to rehearse it to perfection, staying on in the empty Colston Hall after a three-hour session "just once more, to get it right". This was to be Aubrey's last recording as a soloist; an accident the Christmas of that same year put a tragic end to his career as a soloist. Had it not been for the accident we would undoubtedly now possess many more fine recordings, including perhaps the Ethel Smyth Concerto which still remains unrecorded.

As the RAF Orchestra became established during the winter of 1940–1 the daily routine fell into a regular pattern that allowed sufficient free time for outside engagements. Roll-call was at 8.45 am; there followed a three-hour rehearsal interrupted only by a break for tea and 'wads' (slices of thick, soggy bread which Dennis, with no sense of smell and little of taste, consumed in large quantities, much to everyone's disgust!). After the morning rehearsal the players were free unless they were listed for duties or there was a concert by the Band or Orchestra. Invariably they would adjourn to 'Pam's Pantry' for lunch, where Dennis had a standing order for two helpings of everything. This restaurant (now, alas, a launderette) became a kind of concert agency; there was a telephone behind the counter and most of the London agents had the number. Nearly every day a meal was interrupted by Barbara, the waitress, calling someone from his table to answer a call about a concert engagement. Passes were needed for such engagements and were liable to be cancelled without notice. In the majority of cases they were freely granted, however, and often the arrangements for these and for other details such as travel and accommodation were handled by the organization concerned. One such was ENSA, whose headquarters were at the Theatre Royal, Drury Lane. Head of their Music Division was Walter Legge; his dealings with the RAF players during the war years gave him many valuable contacts when, as artists' manager for Columbia Records, he came to form his own orchestra after the end of the war.

The first eighteen months of the war produced very little in the way of orchestral music in London. Players of Dennis's calibre did have one valuable outlet for their talents, however—the National Gallery concerts, founded and organized by Myra Hess. As early as the end of September 1939 she had approached Kenneth Clark, the Gallery's Director, asking him to explore the possibility of using the National Gallery for concerts. When permission had been given and the Home Office ban on crowds using public buildings lifted, Myra Hess and her colleagues set to work. Their aim was two-fold—to present the complete literature of chamber music to the public at a price they could afford and to give promising young musicians the chance to appear beside established artists before a ready-made audience. A flat-rate token fee was paid to all performers—Myra Hess relied on the co-operation of the entire musical profession, and she got it. She gave the first concert herself, on 10 October 1939 before an audience of over a thousand. The Home Office had given permission for two hundred to attend.

Myra Hess and her committee—Kenneth Clark and Frank Howes—planned the programmes a month in advance; the agents, Messrs Ibbs and Tillett, then booked the artists and arranged printing and advertising. The concerts were held at 1.00 pm every weekday (an experiment to repeat Thursday's and Friday's programmes at 4.30 pm was dropped after two and a half months).

The admission charge was one shilling and any profits were given to the Musicians' Benevolent Fund, which received a total of £16,000 between October 1939 and April 1946. Not all the money came from admission charges; £4,000 came in donations from the USA alone—from, among others, Toscanini, Koussevitsky, Rachmaninov and Heifetz.

In line with the aim of providing a comprehensive programme of chamber and orchestral music of all types a number of 'series' concerts were performed—all the Bach Brandenburg Concertos, all the Mozart Piano Concertos, the Bach '48' Preludes and Fugues, and all Beethoven's piano and chamber works.

The RAF Orchestra appeared at the National Gallery a number of times in its entirety, with Dennis as first horn; he also appeared with them as soloist, in Mozart's Fourth Horn Concerto, on 6 April 1942. In fact Dennis made no less than twenty-six solo appearances at the National Gallery in a wide range of works. The Brahms Trio op. 40 for violin, horn and piano was a favourite item, and he played with violinists such as Sidney Griller, Harry Blech and Max Rostal, and with pianists Franz Osborn, Denis Matthews and, on one occasion, with Myra Hess herself. He also joined the Griller Quartet to play the Mozart K 407 Horn Quintet on 5 December 1941, during the Mozart Festival Week in celebration of the hundred and fiftieth anniversary of the composer's death. A comparison of the personnel list of the RAF Orchestra with the National Gallery programmes makes it abundantly clear that the RAF possessed a wealth of talent which it could, and did, provide at every opportunity.

In October 1942 Dennis was given his first post as principal horn with a professional orchestra. It was with a body of players originally known as the 'Sidney Beer Orchestra' but now named the National Symphony Orchestra. Sidney Beer, its conductor and founder, was a somewhat unorthodox musical figure. Born in Liverpool of wealthy parents, he had been educated at Uppingham and Magdalen College, Oxford. Though his family was undoubtedly musically inclined, it did not possess outstanding ability; Sidney played the violin, but his ruling passion from his days at college was racehorses. They consumed both his time and his money until, at the age of thirty-two, in 1931, he enrolled at the Royal College of Music to study conducting with Sargent.

He later studied at the Salzburg Mozarteum, where he first conducted in September 1932, and by the outbreak of the war he had conducted in Vienna, Prague, Berlin and at Covent Garden. When he arrived in London in 1940 after a long spell abroad, he was appalled by the dearth of orchestral music. A burning desire to form an orchestra overruled his caution, for he realized it was a dangerous time to launch any musical venture, let alone a new orchestra. But he had good connections with the Savoy Theatre and succeeded in renting it for a nominal sum. He also obtained the services of an excellent manager, Frederick Laurence, who had managed the London Philharmonic for Beecham before the war. Laurence engaged some very good string-players: members of the Hirsch and Blech Quartets led the sections. The horns were Norman Del Mar and Farquaharson Cousins, but the remaining wind sections were less easy to complete. Many of the best players were tied closely to the BBC Symphony or other orchestras, while some, like Reginald Kell and Leon Goossens, had been given contracts by the BBC at the outset of the war in a 'salon orchestra' at Bristol, ostensibly for the duration of the war. Nevertheless the 'Sidney Beer Orchestra' planned and presented a series of Saturday afternoon concerts during the first three months of 1941. After two concerts at the Savoy Theatre, Beer moved to the Queen's Hall for two more; just two months later, on the night of Saturday 10 May, an incendiary bomb which lodged in the roof destroyed one of London's best-loved concert-halls and birthplace of three of its most famous orchestras.

The Sidney Beer Orchestra was small and by its nature an experiment in wartime music-making. The following winter, Sidney Beer conducted a series of London Philharmonic Orchestra concerts at the Royal Albert Hall. When, in 1942, the BBC disbanded its 'salon orchestra' and many experienced players were released into circulation, Beer was encouraged, with the assistance of his new manager, Victor Olof, to form another, larger orchestra. The wind sections improved considerably. As well as Dennis and Norman Del Mar as first and second horns, Beer now had Arthur Gleghorn and Gareth Morris (flutes), Leon Goossens (oboe), Reginald Kell and Bernard Walton (clarinets) and John Alexandra and Cecil James (bassoons). Leonard Hirsch remained leader. In October 1942 the orchestra began a series of twenty-four Sunday

afternoon concerts at the Phoenix Theatre with a new name—
the National Symphony Orchestra. They made their first appearance at the Royal Albert Hall on 19 January 1943, with Cyril
Smith as the soloist.

Beer had already met Dennis. Finding that he was without a
first horn for one concert which contained a work with a very
exposed solo horn part, he got his manager to telephone Aubrey
Brain in Bristol to find out if he could help. Aubrey was not
available but said: "Tell Mr Beer that I would like to have played
for him, but I will send him one of my pupils and I think he will
find him all right." Sidney Beer waited anxiously for the rehearsal.
When he arrived at the hall he found the first horn chair occupied
by a very young-looking player. He announced that they would
begin and, with a worried glance at the leader, shrugged his
shoulders and started. The horn solo was beautifully played and
after it was over the young player caught Sidney Beer's eye and
gave a shy smile. It was, of course, Dennis, playing for the first
time as principal horn of a London orchestra, just twenty years
old. After the concert, Aubrey rang Sidney Beer and asked, "Was
the boy all right?" The boy was all right. Beer worshipped Dennis
and as time went by Dennis came to like and respect him as a
modest man, a conductor competent enough to start and stop
efficiently but otherwise willing to let the orchestra play what
they knew well.

Inspired by the success of the National Symphony Orchestra,
other orchestras grew up during the war years. One of the finest
was Alec Sherman's New London Orchestra; really a chamber
orchestra, it set a very high standard and was generally busier
than the National Symphony. Myra Hess used it to accompany her
in her series of all the Mozart piano concertos between 1943 and
1945. The New London Orchestra had many familiar faces among
its principals—Leon Goossens, Gareth Morris, Cecil James and
Frederick Thurston—and, not surprisingly, its horns were Dennis
and Norman Del Mar. In fact throughout the war the two of
them were almost inseparable colleagues in every possible group
or combination.

Despite the war, or perhaps because of it, Dennis's reputation
as an outstanding orchestral player and soloist gradually grew in
London's musical life. The flexibility of RAF routine allowed him

to take part in many new ventures; but even the normal demands of everyday service helped to widen his reputation still further by introducing him to the composer Benjamin Britten. In the summer of 1942 a series of commentaries on life in wartime England was broadcast to America. The programmes went out weekly at three o'clock on a Sunday morning. Britten had been commissioned to write the incidental music, which the RAF Orchestra played. At one of the rehearsals Dennis approached Britten over some technical point in a solo passage, and they became friends. Britten recalls that from then on he took every opportunity to write in elaborate solos for the horn! Before very long Dennis had persuaded Britten to write a special work that he could play, and during the ensuing months there gradually evolved, not a horn concerto, but the Serenade op. 31—a series of six poems by English poets set for tenor voice, horn and strings. The RAF rehearsals and broadcasts gave Britten many opportunities to consult Dennis about points of horn technique and phrasing, help which Dennis gladly gave, never rejecting a passage before he had tried it over and over again.

The Serenade received its first performance at the Wigmore Hall, London, on 15 October 1943 by the players for whom it was written—Peter Pears and Dennis, with Walter Goehr conducting. It is a rich and fascinating work and one of the most consistently popular of Britten's earlier compositions. The Prologue and Epilogue which frame the six poems are for horn alone and are directed to be played without the use of valves, that is, using the notes of the natural harmonic series of the horn. As has been mentioned, some of the notes in the series are not quite in tune and at least one critic had evidently not done his homework, for he smugly accused Dennis of faulty intonation! Dennis confided to a friend after a few performances that he wished he had never suggested that the two solos should be played on the natural harmonics. It was his idea originally and Britten thought it a good one. However, Dennis said it was a nuisance to have to explain, in programme notes or personally afterwards why he sounded out of tune. The accompaniments to the poems themselves explore the entire compass of the horn and its full range of dynamic effects; pianissimo top Cs and hand-stopping had all been demonstrated to Britten on those Sunday mornings and were all included in a part that bristles with difficulties but is infinitely rewarding to the listener. Of a performance in Liverpool the northern edition of the *Daily Telegraph* (3 February 1944) wrote:

A work of the first importance which should be heard again soon. The musical ideas flow naturally but the Serenade might have been written for Peter Pears and Dennis Brain so perfectly does it suit them. . . . Mr Brain is a young virtuoso and he concealed the difficulties with as sure a touch as the composer. Earlier in the programme he had played a Mozart concerto with the same ease.

Decca recorded the Serenade on 25 May 1944 with the same artists as had taken part in the 1943 première and with Britten himself conducting. Part of the work was re-recorded on 8 October of the same year. The discs were issued in December 1945 and became a popular addition to Decca's growing classical catalogue. As recently as January 1974 there was an appeal in a gramophone journal for their re-issue, a tribute to the quality of the recording, which captures much of the magic of the early live performances.

Dennis made a number of recordings during the war. Two of them, for Decca, followed National Gallery performances— Howard Ferguson's Octet (National Gallery 17 February 1943) and the Brahms Songs op. 18 (National Gallery 30 December 1943), both rare works which deserve a wider hearing. He also recorded Mozart's Fourth Horn Concerto with the Hallé Orchestra, for Columbia. The conductor should have been Malcolm Sargent but he arrived late for the recording session and the leader, Laurence Turner, took over. The result was so good that Columbia issued it, but they were in something of a dilemma over the exact wording of the record label. The record was finally issued as by 'Dennis Brain with the Hallé Orchestra', which frustrated record collectors, who would want to know the name of the conductor, but solved the problem for Columbia.

The unusually long first movement cadenza for the Mozart concerto recording was written for Dennis by Norman Del Mar. He was a modest but competent composer and spent most of the war working on a colossal opera based on Elroy Flecker's verse play *Hassan*. Dennis and Gareth Morris frequently teased him about it. 'He's a composer, you know,' Dennis would whisper audibly, with mock respect. Not that any of this fooling was ill meant or ill taken. Dennis's quaint, almost boyish innocent sense of humour was the one quality that held the three of them together; inseparable companions in and out of barracks, their sense of fun made them immensely popular and they became known as 'The Three Musketeers'. Norman was often the butt of Dennis's jokes but had little difficulty in obtaining his revenge. It was as well that the friendship survived; Norman's parents lived nearby and frequently invited Dennis and his friends to meals. Dennis's love of food was by now legendary. He had an enormous appetite, as had his father, but his figure suffered considerably more from it as he found particular delight in the more fattening foods. On an RAF tour at Oswestry he ran up to the waiting coach and called in the door: "Gareth, I've found a super restaurant with milk and doughnuts!" Edward Walker, second flute in the RAF Orchestra, turned to Gareth with apparent disgust. "How can someone like that be a true musician?" he sighed.

The Mozart concerto had been recorded in June 1943. In the following April Dennis made another recording for Columbia, which is still in their catalogue. It was of the Beethoven Horn Sonata op. 17, which he and Denis Matthews recorded in RAF uniform. This marked the beginning of Dennis's permanent association with Columbia (later EMI) records; he had made the Mozart recording under a letter of agreement but with the Beethoven he took on an exclusive contract, renewable every year. Denis Matthews recalls the recording as a happy artistic collaboration. "To play such a piece with Dennis was both a privilege and a pleasure. He was a wonderful ensemble player—a gift which does not always go with virtuosity. Somehow he had that rare instinctive musicianship and flexibility of phrase which always adapted itself to the musical environment of the moment." Perhaps one clue as to why such an old recording of a rather hurriedly written composition should survive in these days of quadrophonic sound can be found in the *Scotsman*'s review of a performance given by Dennis in 1950 of the same work:

It is said of Dennis Brain that he makes horn-playing appear as if there were no technical problems whatever, but he improves on this by the first-rate artistry with which he illuminates his technique. In the case of the Beethoven Sonata op. 17 he made it appear a far more significant work than it really is.

With such manifest skill and musicianship it was natural that Dennis would be wooed by any new groups which sprang up during the war years. Two new ensembles that emerged from the National Gallery concerts were the London Wind Players and the London Baroque Ensemble, both of which unhesitatingly appointed Dennis as first horn.

In August 1942 Myra Hess had asked Harry Blech to form a wind group to perform all the Mozart and Beethoven serenades for wind instruments. Blech, a founder member of the BBC Symphony Orchestra and whose own string quartet (formed in 1935) had not only provided the basis of the National Symphony Orchestra but had recently had the distinction of giving the first performance of Walton's String Quartet, was also a member of the RAF Orchestra; it was from there that he inevitably drew many of his players. At the London Wind Players' first concert, on 19 August 1942, Dennis, Norman Del Mar, Vivian Grey and Livia Gollancz were the four horns in Mozart's B♭ Divertimento K 361 which formed the main part of the programme. A second Mozart concert on 18 December was so successful that it had to be repeated 'by special request' on 26 January 1943. The London Wind Players flourished, with more concerts at the National Gallery and the Churchill Club. Decca invited them to record another Mozart divertimento, K 166 in E major, and this as well as some broadcasts helped to establish a wide following for the ensemble and its players.

The London Baroque Ensemble dated from 1941, when Karl Haas had collected a small group of players to broadcast some early string music. Haas was ex-Director of Music for Stuttgart Radio and had fled to Britain in June 1939 in the face of growing Nazi persecution. He had brought with him many rare musical instruments which, unhappily, he had been forced to sell in order to maintain himself. He was able to keep some five thousand microfilms of rare music for both strings and wind which he had collected over the years from various continental libraries. For four years he gave his main attention to string music, and a Wigmore Hall concert in 1943 and a series of eight National Gallery concerts in the winter of 1944–5 followed the early broadcasts. By now Haas wanted to give more attention to music for wind instruments. He maintained that "British wind players are unequalled in the whole world", a view no doubt strengthened by appearances at the National Gallery by the London Wind Players and soloists such as Dennis. After the RAF Orchestra returned from the United States in 1945 he gathered together as many of the best wind-players as he could and on 26 June presented a Haydn and Mozart programme at the National Gallery: Haydn's F major Divertimento for wind, a Sonata for violin and viola by Haydn and Mozart's Sextet in B♭ for wind K 270. Dennis was again supported by Norman Del Mar in this interesting début.

But music for Dennis did not consist entirely of Mozart and Haydn, nor was it exclusively classical. He was passionately fond of jazz and never missed an opportunity to take an active part in it. Both he and Norman turned up in every conceivable type of dance band and with his natural versatility Dennis was often called upon to try out a new jazz arrangement. One band in particular claimed his allegiance—Geraldo's—and many were the nights that he and Norman would creep into the pit and join in for a couple of hours. At that time, towards the end of the war, Geraldo had a large concert orchestra and could make room for two horns; for fun they once did an arrangement of "Where in the World". Dennis had only one reservation about playing the horn in jazz arrangements: the horn was so similar in tone to the tenor trombone that it could not compete with it as a serious jazz instrument.

Summer 1944 saw the end of Dennis and Leonard's stay in Uxbridge. Leonard had already got married and was the first to move away, but when in early 1944 the quarters in Uxbridge were bombed Dennis had to look elsewhere for accommodation. He found a house in Elsworthy Terrace, Swiss Cottage, where he shared rooms with the violinist, Thomas Carter. With his shy, rather naïve character, Dennis had made very few romantic attachments, but that summer he met a young pianist studying at the Royal Academy, Yvonne Coles. The daughter of a Petersfield accountant, Yvonne was five years younger than Dennis: a tiny, attractive girl, she was also very shy. She was a talented pianist, a pupil of Harold Craxton, and had performed the Brahms Second Piano Concerto with the Academy Orchestra. Dennis first noticed her at the Academy one afternoon as he was chatting with Denis Matthews in the entrance hall and asked if he knew who she was. By chance, Denis Matthews was at that time taking some of Harold Craxton's lessons for him and was able to tell Dennis a little about

her. They soon met and became a devoted pair, with a simple enjoyment of life, a common love of music and an utter reliance on
each other's company. Within a year they were engaged, soon after
Dennis's return from the RAF's tour of the United States.

The RAF Orchestra and Band left for their tour, a goodwill
trip arranged as an exchange with the Band of the US Army Air
Force, late in 1944. For the RAF, the prospect of visiting some of
the more famous cities in the USA coupled with the chance to
enjoy ration-free food and drink was attractive, to say the least.
No less than 104 musicians assembled at Euston Station on 30
November: with them were Wing-Commander O'Donnell and
assistant conductor Pilot Officer John Hollingsworth. The company
made its way via Morecambe to Gourock on the Clyde where they
were taken on board the *Queen Mary*. They found the ship only
one third full and RAF personnel were drafted in to augment the
ship's staff, an arrangement that caused no little resentment. However, a number of concerts by the Band and the Orchestra helped
to smooth the crossing, and on the morning of 8 December Dennis
saw the famous New York skyline for the first time as the *Queen
Mary* steamed into the Hudson River. No sooner had they docked
than a fleet of buses whisked them away to Camp Kilmer, New
Brunswick, where they spent the next two nights. Most of their
time was their own but New York had been put out of bounds.
Next stop was Washington where they were billeted in the Army
Air Force quarters of the band making the exchange tour of
Britain. Here they were allowed to go sight-seeing and rehearsals
began for the first concert, to be given in Constitution Hall on
18 December. A large audience, which included General Arnold,
Chief-of-Staff US Army Air Force, and Lord Halifax, the British
Ambassador, gave a warm reception to a very mixed programme
of pieces by Sullivan, Coates, Tchaikovsky, Smetana and Elgar, as
well as a most unusual arrangement of Bach's D minor Toccata
and Fugue. After the concert both the Band and Orchestra stayed
on to play seven more items which NBC relayed direct from the
hall to its radio network; everyone was tired and O'Donnell managed to conduct both the *Swan Lake* and Serenade waltzes two
in a bar!

The critics in the *Washington Post* and the *Times Herald* were
guardedly polite, but the same programme was repeated on the

following day before an enthusiastic audience. Earlier in the day Dennis had gone with the Griller Quartet and Max Gilbert to a British Officers' Club in the city to play the Mozart K 407 Horn Quintet. They were well fed and entertained but after one movement of the Quintet, Sidney Griller refused to continue playing as the audience seemed to be quite unaware of their presence. This total lack of manners put an end to one of the few chances Dennis had on the tour to play as a soloist.

The tour itself brought its share of trials for all the players. The continual migration from camp to camp by 'bus, lorry and train was just bearable but exceedingly tiring. There were countless concerts, held in a weird assortment of locales ranging from Methodist church halls to open-air bandstands; one was in a large hangar where the audience was seated so far away they were almost out of sight and there was an eight-second echo. What became increasingly obvious, though, was O'Donnell's insensitivity to the finer points of musicianship. High though his aspirations had been at the outset of the war in forming the RAF Orchestra, he was a bandsman at heart and made no secret of the fact that he had little respect for string-players. In Atlantic City he lost his temper and succeeded in breaking his glasses, while in Miami he not only tried to catch out the strings in *Eine Kleine Nachtmusik* by sudden changes of tempo but, seeing the nicely printed programme that had been prepared, also asserted his individuality by changing every item.

He was in fine humour, however, for the concert in Nassau, which was attended by the Duke and Duchess of Windsor. Whether his mood could be attributed to the presence of such distinguished guests or to the fact that he had flown from Miami in fifty-five minutes (leaving the Band to come by boat in eighteen hours) is a matter for conjecture.

A crisis came one wet day in San Antonio, Texas. The day's rehearsal was abruptly ended after only five minutes and there followed a lecture by O'Donnell on the general lines of "I am a Wing-Commander: discipline never hurt anyone intelligent enough to accept it in the right spirit; I shall be glad to get rid of you, the strings are contaminating the band, etc." It made relations very uncomfortable and when in Phoenix the string-players asked to keep their instruments out of the hot sun and in the shade of the bandstand in which they were playing O'Donnell threatened to send them all back to Washington. Strangely the incident seemed to clear away much of the tension; the strains of travelling and enforced proximity had taken time to come to the boil, and the heat had at last gone.

There were many compensations. The food was superb and at nearly every camp parties were thrown specially for the Band by their American hosts. With typical generosity free passes and tickets to a vast number of functions were always made available and there was a good deal of free time to enjoy these and the pleasures of such resorts as Miami and Nassau. For Dennis the highlight of the tour was undoubtedly their visit to Los Angeles, where they arrived on 26 January 1945. Now he had the chance to meet his Uncle Alfred, for whom he had a great deal of respect both as a horn-player and as a person. Dennis had looked forward eagerly to the meeting, and the RAF's schedule for the four-day stay in Los Angeles was not very full—a dance at the Mirama Hotel, a concert in Santa Monica on the 26th, visits to the film studios of MGM and Twentieth-Century Fox, and a couple more concerts.

Dennis and Leonard spent nearly all the four days with Al. On their first day they went for tea and in the evening Al and Straussie took them out to dinner at the 'Tropics' in Los Angeles. As they sat talking afterwards Al took the opportunity to give Dennis one of his mouthpieces to use.

"There are not many players who can use this type of mouthpiece," Al told him, "but I think it will suit you."

It was a very small, thin-rimmed conical brass mouthpiece and Dennis used it almost exclusively for the rest of his life. He had a great deal in common with his uncle, besides physical similarity and common horn technique. They both had a good-humoured, outgoing personality, almost the complete antithesis of Aubrey's more sedate, serious-minded temperament.

On the following day they were taken round Al's chicken farm; he gave them the day's takings, over a hundred dollars, to spend on themselves in Los Angeles. That evening there was a party at Al's house to which he invited not only Dennis, Leonard and Gareth Morris but most of the horn-players in the Los Angeles area as well. Leonard remembered the party as a "sea of alcohol";

it lasted from 6 pm to 6 am the following day, and Al never allowed any party to run 'dry'. One end of the large living-room had been set up as a huge bar. About midnight Dennis's piston-valved horn was produced and everyone tried, with little success, to produce a note on it. To the American players it looked like a museum-piece and after they had all had a go Dennis was persuaded to demonstrate. Without a word he took it and played a section from "The Flight of the Bumble-Bee".

"Not a bad instrument," he smiled, handing it back. The party exploded.

Dennis treasured his recollections of the stay in Los Angeles for many years to come. His fabulous technique and boyish ways endeared him to the horn-playing community there and laid the foundations of his reputation which still remains.

The rest of the tour was almost an anticlimax. The long journey back overland to Washington by way of Denver and Omaha passed without too many incidents. O'Donnell had to hand over the baton to John Hollingsworth for several concerts as he had sustained a leg injury, but he was sufficiently recovered to conduct again in Constitution Hall, Washington on 26 February. On the next day they were back in New York, and this time they were allowed to see the sights, in between giving two concerts and an official broadcast. For Dennis and Gareth the temptation of a good meal and the chance to hear a top American jazz band took them to the '400' Club where Tommy Dorsey was playing. They both met him after the show and to Dennis's delight and amazement he had heard of both Alfred and Aubrey and admired their playing. Dorsey treated them to drinks and they talked for some time; Dennis was delighted to find him as charming a person as he was fabulous a player.

Less than a week later the whole Band and Orchestra were back in England after a tour of twelve thousand miles through twenty-eight states. The tour had done much to increase the reputation of British musicians in America, though O'Donnell had confirmed the Americans' worst fears about the Englishman's eccentricity. Stresses and strains of touring had taken a heavy toll however, and there was never again the same musical or personal unity within the RAF Band and Orchestra.

In London the National Gallery concerts were still running,

and Myra Hess was nearing the end of her series of Mozart piano concertos. Within a month Dennis was playing at the Gallery again in a Mozart recital by the London Wind Players, and there were more concerts there until the early part of 1946. Life seemed to be normal, but feverish preparations for post-war musical life were in hand.

Some of the principals of the National Symphony Orchestra, with their conductor, Sidney Beer (seated centre) and leader, Leonard Hirsch (standing), October 1942. On the left are Arthur Gleghorn (flute) and Bernard Walton (clarinet); Dennis Brain is on the far right. (*photo: Radio Times Hulton Picture Library*)

Alf Brain with Dennis and Leonard at Alf's chicken farm during the R.A.F. tour of America, January 1945. (*photo: courtesy Mrs Alfred Brain*)

Dennis's wedding photograph, Petersfield, 8 September 1945. On the far left is Gareth Morris, Dennis's best man, and on the far right Leonard and his wife. (*photo: courtesy Mrs Alfred Brain*)

The horns of the Royal Philharmonic Orchestra recording Strauss's "Ein Heldenleben" with Beecham, November 1947. With Dennis are Ian Beers (hidden), Roy White, Frank Probyn, Edmund Chapman, Mark Foster, Alf Cursue and H. Hamilton. (*photo: Press Illustrations*)

ஃ 6 ௸

First Horn: the Breakthrough

The end of the Second World War found England with a pool of outstanding players from which any enterprising impresario might build up a first-class orchestra. Dennis's performances as a member of the RAF Orchestra and as a soloist had assured him of a prominent place in post-war musical life. As early as 1944 an editorial in *Music Review* had commented:

We have five pianists of the first rank in Curzon, Stadlen, Kentner, Solomon, and Myra Hess—and two more deserving of systematic encouragement: Noel Mewton-Wood and Denis Matthews; two outstanding violinists in Henry Holst and Max Rostal; and Frederick Riddle (viola), Douglas Cameron (cello), Leon Goossens (oboe) and Dennis Brain (horn), who should be given more frequent opportunity for appearance as soloists with orchestras.

With such a reputation, Dennis was certain of obtaining one of the choice posts in the London orchestras. During the RAF's American tour he had received an offer from Leopold Stokowski to go to Philadelphia as first horn there 'when the war was over' but, whether he wanted to go or not, he was still tied to the RAF until September 1946. Long before then a number of exciting developments had ensured that he would stay in England.

Ironically, an unfortunate accident early in the war had made Dennis's future even more secure than otherwise it might have been. On Christmas Day 1940 his father Aubrey was returning to his quarters in Bristol after visiting his wife who was staying in a hotel in Burnham-on-Sea. In the blackout he missed his footing on the icy promenade and fell, fracturing the neck of his right femur. It was some considerable time before he was found and taken to the local hospital where, underestimating the seriousness of the injury, the understaffed orthopaedic department insisted on patching up the leg themselves. Back in Bristol, Aubrey continued playing but he remained in some pain. As soon as possible he took the advice of a consultant at the Bristol Infirmary and underwent an operation known as 'Murray's Osteotomy', in which the neck of the femur is reset, thus easing the tension on the distorted hip-joint. The operation was a success, except that his right leg was now one inch shorter than the left. He was in high spirits, however, when he wrote to Clarence Raybould, the chief assistant conductor of the BBC Symphony Orchestra, in the summer of 1942 during convalescence at the Orthopaedic Hospital at Winford, near Bristol: "I am not looking forward to learning the horn all over again, but as I have some idea of it, and how to play, perhaps it won't be as bad as anticipated . . . am amusing myself making belts from string. . . ."

By the time Aubrey left Winford the BBC Symphony Orchestra had moved to Bedford, since repeated air-raids had made Bristol too uncomfortable. He rejoined the orchestra, playing for a time with his old flair and skill. Boult even arranged for him to go to London for a week to help out the London Symphony Orchestra and Aubrey was warmly thanked for his "kindly interest in the orchestra's struggle to maintain a front-rank position". But towards the end of the war Aubrey began to suffer blurred vision, slurring of his speech and tingling sensations in his fingers and toes—all early symptoms of disseminated sclerosis. At the first 1945 Prom rehearsal, on 21 July, he was taken ill and had to retire from full-time playing, while still in his early fifties.

Thus, Dennis was spared having to compete with his own father for supremacy in the London orchestral world. He was not, however, successful in replacing his father as principal horn in the BBC Symphony: Aubrey Thonger won that distinction after auditions in the late autumn of 1945.

Dennis became involved in the first post-war orchestra to be formed in London, the Philharmonia, founded primarily for recording by Walter Legge, who was artists' manager of the Columbia Graphophone Company and head of the Music Division of ENSA. Legge had formed a string quartet early in 1941 consisting of Henry Holst, Jean Pougnet, Frederick Riddle and Anthony Pini. He rehearsed them every weekend and then recorded the

Mozart "Hunt" Quartet K 458. The quartet was given the title 'Philharmonia' and the success of the Mozart and subsequent recordings was so great that they were asked to perform the complete Beethoven quartets, first in Birmingham and later in Liverpool in the summer of 1944. David Wise replaced Jean Pougnet as second violin and Herbert Downes came in as viola. The four were appointed leaders of the string sections of the Liverpool Philharmonic Orchestra, which had managed to secure many of the outstanding players who had not found their way into the services.

In 1944 Walter Legge arranged a Wigmore Hall concert by the Philharmonia Quartet which was completely sold out. Reginald Kell was then invited to join them to perform the Mozart and Brahms Clarinet Quintets, later recording the Mozart Quintet with them. Within a few weeks the 'Quartet' had grown to seven for the Ravel Septet. Towards the end of the war Legge began to put his long-laid plans into action: he would form a first-class orchestra of young musicians, assuring them of work before they were demobilized. Early in 1945 he engaged twenty-four strings from the RAF Orchestra to make a series of recordings of works by Purcell and Sibelius. More followed, and wind-players were brought in for such works as Bartók's Roumanian Dances, Walton's Sinfonia Concertante and the Tchaikovsky B♭ minor Piano Concerto with Moiseiwitsch. The wind-players were also mainly chosen from the RAF Orchestra, and Dennis was the first principal horn.

Although the records had a rather lukewarm reception, Legge together with Victor Schuster formed the Philharmonia Concert Society. Four Saturday afternoon concerts at the Wigmore Hall were arranged for July 1945: the Philharmonia Quartet played two Beethoven Quartets on 7 July, Denis Matthews, Henry Holst and Anthony Pini gave a programme of trios on the 14th and a week later there was a Mozart concert that included the Trio for clarinet, viola and piano and the Clarinet Quintet, at which the conductor, Walter Susskind, played the piano in place of Denis Matthews who was ill. Dennis Brain was due to play at the last of the four concerts in Beethoven's Sonata op. 17 and the Brahms Trio, but the programme had to be revised as the RAF Orchestra and Band were flown out to Potsdam for a group of concerts to

be given during the conference. There were three Potsdam con-
certs: on 20 July at the British Delegation, on 23 July at the Prime
Minister's house and on 24 July in the New Palace of Sans Souci.
Dennis was away for a week and he returned to find Legge and
Schuster busy with plans for the 1945–6 season; the success of the
July concerts had encouraged them to plan five autumn concerts in
Kingsway Hall. The first concert, on 27 October, would mark
the public début of the Philharmonia Orchestra and was to be
conducted by Sir Thomas Beecham.

The interval between the trip to Potsdam and the Philharmonia's
début gave Dennis and Yvonne the ideal opportunity to make
final plans for their wedding, and on 8 September they were
married in the Parish Church at Petersfield, Hampshire. Leonard
and his wife were there, but Aubrey unfortunately was still too ill
to be able to attend. Gareth Morris was best man, and he and
Dennis drove down to Petersfield together, stopping at a local
hotel for lunch.

"I think I need something strong to drink," Dennis confided
to Gareth. "How about a sherry?" When the sherries were brought
Dennis immediately succeeded in knocking his over. "Another,
sir?" enquired the waiter as he mopped up the first. Dennis
grinned: "Just a glass of water this time."

Dennis and Gareth were both in RAF uniform for the occasion
and it gave an air of ceremony to the service. After the reception
Dennis and Yvonne drove up to London for their honeymoon.
They then moved into the bungalow they had bought at Hayes,
Middlesex. Though some way from the centre of London, it was
near to the RAF at Uxbridge, and Dennis now returned to his RAF
commitments. On 27 October, the Philharmonia Orchestra's long-
awaited début took place in Kingsway Hall. About forty of the
fifty-two players were soldiers or airmen. The programme was all-
Mozart: Symphony no. 40 in G minor, the Clarinet Concerto (with
Reginald Kell), the Divertimento in D K 131 and the Six German
Dances K 604. The quality of the performance delighted not only
the audience but the guest conductor, Sir Thomas Beecham, who
declared: "The privilege of directing this magnificent concert of
artists is such that my pleasure would be diminished if I accepted
a fee. I would, however, gladly accept a cigar."

He received a whole box of cigars when he dined with Walter

Legge the following Monday and at once declared his intention of making the Philharmonia *his* orchestra. Before returning to England from the USA in 1944 Beecham had openly declared his ambitions to form 'one more orchestra'. But Legge would have none of it. As early as 1942 he had drawn up a code by which he resolved to run the Philharmonia Orchestra. It read:

1. There are enough first-class orchestral players scattered about Britain to make one orchestra at least equal, and in many ways superior, to the best of any European country. All these players must be in one orchestra—the Philharmonia.

2. It would be an orchestra of such quality that the best instrumentalists would compete for the honour of playing in it.

3. No 'passengers'. One inferior player can mar a whole orchestra's intonation and ensemble.

4. An orchestra which consists only of artists distinguished in their own right can give of its best only in co-operation with the best conductors.

5. No 'permanent' conductor. A 'one-man-band' inevitably bears the mark of its permanent conductor's personality, his own particular sonority and his approach to music. The Philharmonia Orchestra should have style, not 'a style'.

Walter Legge remained firmly and politely faithful to this last stipulation and Beecham, piqued, took his box of cigars and began to lay plans elsewhere.

If we look at the list of principals for that first concert we can see that Legge was equally faithful to his demands for the 'best instrumentalists'. Leader was Leonard Hirsch, and the remaining string sections were led by Gerald Emms, Max Gilbert, James Whitehead and J. W. Merrett. Other principals were Arthur Gleghorn (flute), Alec Whittaker (oboe), Reginald Kell (clarinet), John Alexandra (bassoon), Harry Mortimer (trumpet) and James Bradshaw (tympani). The original horn section of the orchestra consisted of Dennis, his RAF friend and colleague Norman Del Mar, Alan Hyde and Frank Probyn, and they all received an appreciative grin from Beecham at the opening concert as he launched them into the Horn Quartet which forms the Minuet of the Mozart D major Divertimento.

Dennis was still in the RAF but the Philharmonia's early work was sporadic enough to allow him to cope. There were more recordings and the remaining concerts in the chamber-music series planned for the autumn. Dennis took part in one of these, on 17 November in Kingsway Hall, in a performance of the Mozart Piano and Wind Quintet. He was also the soloist in the second of two further Kingsway Hall orchestral concerts in early 1946. Walter Legge had engaged John Barbirolli to conduct both and on 9 February Dennis played in an orchestral programme that included the Nocturne from Mendelssohn's *Midsummer Night's Dream*. For the concert on 23 March Barbirolli was ill, and Susskind again came to the rescue, this time to conduct, with Dennis as soloist in Mozart's Third Concerto. They both recorded Mozart's Second Concerto for Columbia later in the same month. Columbia offered Dennis a choice of a composite fee (about £10) or the royalties on sales of the records. Still inexperienced in the financial intricacies of recording, Dennis took the fee. It was a mistake, for the records sold extremely well and he could have earned a great deal more than he did. He was not a man to be careless about money. Although he lost many opportunities to raise his income, refusing to join his fellow principals in the Philharmonia when they were pressing for higher fees, he was nevertheless naturally cautious. The story is told that in an orchestral sweepstake he agreed to put a couple of shillings on a horse until he was told that he would lose his money if the horse did not run, let alone win. Dennis promptly withdrew, pouring scorn on such futile pastimes!

Dennis recorded the Mozart concerto on his usual instrument, but he now used a B♭ crook and had had the valve slides shortened accordingly. He was becoming more and more convinced that the B♭ horn was the most suitable for solo work, of which he was doing an increasing amount. Even his father had reluctantly resorted to a B♭ horn for certain works, and Dennis was doing far more than his father. The Raoux was now showing its age: there were numerous dents and some of the stays were held together with bits of chewing-gum and insulating tape!

On 25 March 1946, shortly before leaving for Germany with the RAF, Dennis took part in one of the last National Gallery concerts. It was with the London Baroque Ensemble and contained some interesting works, all of which were receiving their first London performances: wind sonatas and a clarinet duo by C. P. E.

Bach, and Haydn's Marches for the Prince of Wales and for the Derbyshire Volunteer Cavalry. Dennis and Norman Del Mar played in both the wind sonatas and the marches, but the last work in the concert featured Dennis as soloist in the first performance of a work that is something of a showpiece for the horn, Haydn's Divertimento in E♭ for horn, violin and cello. David Martin and William Pleeth joined him in a work that bristles with difficulties of every kind: pedal notes, rapid demi-semiquavers, octave leaps and scales rising as high as the seventeenth harmonic.

While Dennis was in Germany during April 1946 his own Wind Quintet gave its first concert. He had formed the group mainly from his friends in the RAF and the Royal Academy believing that if this type of music were properly rehearsed it could be made to sound just as appealing as any other. The very real danger that the ear will quickly tire of the sound of wind instruments can be overcome if the players recognize the hidden nuances of the music. Dennis chose players who could do this. His brother Leonard was oboist, Gareth Morris flautist and Tom Wightman bassoonist; Stephen Waters was chosen as clarinettist since Alwyn Kell, with whom the others had performed so happily during their Academy days, had been killed during the war. At the first concert, given before the Chelsea Music Club in Chelsea Town Hall on 30 April 1946, Norman Del Mar played horn in Dennis's absence. The concert was well received but the quintet had to wait until Dennis and Leonard were free of the RAF before they could really get busy. They did, however, manage to give their first broadcast on 26 September, with Dennis this time, in Hindemith's *Kleine Kammermusik*.

While he was still in the RAF Dennis had become increasingly interested in cars and motoring generally. During the war he and Leonard had shared CPJ 815, an extremely reliable two-seater open Morris 8. At the end of the war Dennis bought an Austin 7 which he used almost exclusively, although at about the same time he also acquired a Morgan 4–4 which had the alarming habit of opening its radiator when it went over a bump! Dennis travelled a lot by car: he found it the most convenient form of transport as well as the most relaxing. Motoring was a hobby which he indulged by collecting cars rather than repairing them. Soon after the Morgan he also bought a 21 h.p. Talbot which was fitted with a Wilson gearbox and gave a great deal of mechanical trouble.

The Philharmonia season continued in the spring of 1946 with six appearances by the pianist Arthur Schnabel. Three of these were with the Philharmonia Orchestra at the Royal Albert Hall and included all the Beethoven piano concertos, as well as the Triple Concerto (with Arthur Grumiaux and Pierre Fournier). Two of these concerts were conducted by Issay Dobrowen and one by Alceo Galliera; they undoubtedly added a great deal to the prestige of the Philharmonia which had primarily been formed to make gramophone recordings. Such success irked Beecham, who had fruitlessly tried to restore his old relationship with the London Philharmonic Orchestra. With his noted persistence he resolved to form a completely new orchestra of his own. In August 1946 he took a suite of rooms and a two-room office at the Waldorf Hotel and with Victor Olof, the manager of the new orchestra, set about engaging his players. Often a telephone call or a telegram was sufficient and within three and a half weeks a total of ninety-six players was available. Beecham intended normal working size to be eighty and on 13 September he was able to outline his plans to the press. The name of the orchestra—the Royal Philharmonic—caused no little stir within the highly revered society that had borne that name for over thirty years. Undaunted, Beecham announced that the Royal Philharmonic, led by John Pennington, was assured of thirty concerts before Christmas, a total of seventy-four paid engagements including gramophone sessions and rehearsals. A £3000 advance on gramophone royalties helped to finance the RPO as did, later, income from films and from the Delius Trust.

The players Beecham assembled for the first rehearsal, in St Pancras Town Hall, just four days before the concert, contained some very inexperienced and modest instrumentalists in the rank-and-file but the woodwind principals left nothing to be desired—Peter Newbury, Gerald Jackson, Reginald Kell and Archie Camden. Nor had Beecham skimped in his choice of brass players, notably the horns. "The horn quartet," he told the press, "will be the finest in Europe. First horn, Dennis Brain, is a prodigy." The remainder of the horn quartet in fact differed only in one member from that of the Philharmonia—Roy White was third horn instead of Alan Hyde. Thus at 3 pm on Sunday 15 September Dennis took his place in the Davis Theatre, Croydon, for the début of the second great London orchestra in which he was to lead the horns. He now had very little incentive to leave Britain, for the USA or anywhere else.

The RPO's first concert can be said to have firmly established Dennis's career. Though several months were to elapse before the orchestra emerged as a force to be reckoned with, certainly internationally, from then on Dennis's solo and orchestral engagements began to fall into some kind of regular pattern, interspersed with the now regular recording sessions. Only four days after the Croydon concert Dennis was back in Kingsway Hall for the first concert of the Philharmonia's 1946–7 season. Walter Susskind was again conducting, and again Dennis appeared as soloist in Mozart's Third Concerto in E♭ K 447. Denis Matthews, who played Beethoven's "Emperor" Concerto in the same concert, remembers that Dennis was apprehensive at playing this concerto from memory for the first time. The *Daily Telegraph*'s notice demonstrated that his fears were groundless:

> Dennis Brain played one of Mozart's horn concertos with a truly wonderful beauty of tone and technical assurance and one asked 'was anything like such horn-playing known a generation ago?'

The latter part of October 1946 was taken up with a tour of Britain by the Boyd Neel Orchestra organized by Decca to promote sales of their recent recordings of all the Bach Brandenburg Concertos. Nearly a dozen large towns and cities were visited. At each all the concertos were performed in two concerts. The London performances were at the Chelsea Town Hall and the *Observer* remarked that "they approached perfection as near as any earthly performances ever will". The team of players was certainly star-studded, including Leon Goossens, Gareth Morris, Archie Camden and George Eskdale. Dennis and Norman Del Mar played the horn parts for the Concerto no. 1 (their names do not appear on the record labels as Dennis was under contract to EMI) and they had enormous fun at the recording sessions. Despairing of the phrase-marks on the music that was supplied, Dennis managed to find a book of studies that quoted the parts almost in their entirety from an arrangement Bach had made for a cantata. With some modifications and the addition of some sensible phrasing they were used instead.

Back in London, Dennis's time was immediately occupied with the RPO. Beecham had planned a Delius Festival, a series of seven concerts the first of which, on 26 October, would mark the London début of the RPO. The orchestra was to play at all the concerts except the last on 11 December, when the BBC Symphony was to perform *A Mass of Life*. Many first performances were given— *Under the Pines, Three Small Tone Poems, Marche Caprice*—and in the solo concertos the soloists were Betty Humby-Beecham (piano), Jean Pougnet and Paul Beard (violins) and Anthony Pini (cello). Some of the works were also recorded shortly afterwards. It was an extremely busy period, but on a day off from the RPO Dennis and Leonard finally obtained demobilization from the RAF after just over seven years' service. There had been congenial times, but lately their ties with the RAF had become more and more tiresome as professional playing made increasing demands on their time.

At one of the Delius Festival rehearsals Dennis and Norman Del Mar approached Beecham to ask him to come to a concert to be held in Chelsea Town Hall on 26 November. Norman had taken over from Boyd Neel an amateur orchestra which met every Monday evening and called itself the Central London Orchestra. It had an unlikely collection of players: there were no violas at all but it could boast a tuba! Norman worked hard, recruiting players and planning concerts at Chelsea Town Hall. The players were mostly students, of modest abilities, but in time standards improved and when Dennis East was appointed leader the orchestra was renamed the Chelsea Symphony Orchestra and as such flourished until the early 1950s. Norman's friendship with Dennis made the inclusion of a horn concerto almost inevitable, and for the 26 November concert the programme included not only the Strauss Concerto no. 1 but a large part of the second act of Wagner's *Siegfried*, in which Dennis played the famous horn-call. When they showed Beecham the posters he said grandly "I will come," and to their delight he did, arriving just as Dennis opened the Strauss concerto with its ringing fanfare. Again the *Daily Telegraph* was quick to respond:

The lovely quality of Mr Brain's tone was a constant delight. That he is the best English horn-player of his time was shown again in an extract from the Second Act of *Siegfried*.

Dennis soon recorded the Strauss concerto, with Alceo Galliera and the Philharmonia. For much of his life Dennis thought that this recording best represented his playing, and the work itself became one of his favourites. "It makes a welcome change from the Mozarts," he once said, "and it really is the greatest fun to play." Other concerts too brought him relief from the Mozarts: for a while he included in his repertoire the Ethel Smyth concerto, which he had played earlier in November 1946 with Frederick Grinke and the Liverpool Philharmonic Orchestra, conducted by Eugene Goossens.

The Wind Quintet was also busy and gave concerts all over the country during the winter of 1946–7. One rather terrifying occasion was in the Wigmore Hall on 4 March 1947. It was the time of the great 'freeze-up': all electricity was turned off except for perhaps an hour in the afternoon. When they were allowed to rehearse there was no heating, they were freezing cold, and the programme included the very difficult Sextet for piano and wind by Poulenc. At the concert Poulenc himself played the piano part, very loudly, and then took all the applause. They also played the Wind Quintet by Roberto Gerhard: at that time they did not know the work too well, and Leonard's wife, who attended the concert, said she had never seen five such worried men—all counting like mad. Later they got to know and enjoy the quintet much more and gave its first broadcast performance in November 1947.

Both the Philharmonia and Royal Philharmonic Orchestras were adding to their public prestige. Schnabel returned for a second series of Philharmonia concerts, while Beecham's success with the Delius Festival and his first recordings encouraged him to engage in sping 1947 such artists as Adolf Busch, Myra Hess, Ginette Neveu and Solomon. One of the RPO's finest achievements was a broadcast on the BBC's new Third Programme of *The Trojans* by Berlioz: relayed on 2 and 4 July 1947 the performances had an incandescent quality that will probably never be equalled again. Much of the credit for this can be attributed to the sheer terror of the players. Beecham was suffering from gout and his temper had worsened as the rehearsals progressed. At the broadcast his look of black fury held the players rigid in their seats, not daring to make the slightest hint of a slip. Of all the outstanding moments of that performance, perhaps the one that remains most vivid is Dennis's playing of the famous solo in the "Royal Hunt and Storm". For Leonard the final bars of that section were one of the most beautiful examples of horn-playing he had ever heard: Dennis, already playing *pianissimo*, was waved down even quieter by Beecham until he was almost inaudible, still maintaining the last note with infallible control.

In common with the many musicians who played in both the RPO and the Philharmonia, Dennis found that he could afford to devote a decreasing amount of time to other orchestras, particularly in view of the demands made on him by solo work and recitals with his quintet. One notable instance was Sidney Beer's National Symphony Orchestra, for which Dennis had played less and less since the war. It had made a very successful tour of Europe in May 1946, on which Dennis could not go, but had then confined its activities largely to gramophone recordings. Sidney Beer spent a great deal of time abroad and consequently the number of records was few—*too* few for Decca who, in September 1947, terminated the Orchestra's recording contract, depriving it of a potential revenue of some £20,000. This was virtually the death-blow for the National Symphony. It struggled on for a while but soon broke up: with such slender financial resources it could not hope to compete with the RPO and the Philharmonia. So ended an orchestra that had given Dennis and many others their first professional engagements and which in its prime had made a significant contribution both to London's wartime music and to the recorded repertoire.

On 25 September 1947 Dennis made his first solo appearance at a major festival. At the Norfolk and Norwich 35th Triennial Festival he and Peter Pears performed the Britten Serenade, with the London Symphony Orchestra and Dr Heathcote Statham. The Serenade had gained wide popularity largely through the recording Dennis made in 1944 but also as a result of regular live performances. Dennis had made it a regular feature of his repertoire, often pairing it with a Mozart concerto in the same programme. The Norfolk and Norwich concert was only the first of a steady procession of festival performances by Dennis. And for the horn it was a major breakthrough as a respectable solo instrument.

The works of Richard Strauss contain a wealth of solo horn parts and it was with a festival of this composer's music that Beecham chose to open a series of RPO concerts at the Theatre Royal, Drury Lane, in the autumn of 1947. The success of the venture was greatly enhanced when Strauss himself, then in his eighty-fourth year, agreed not only to attend the Festival but to conduct one of the concerts. As it happened, Strauss conducted not the RPO but the Philharmonia: Walter Legge had arranged a Royal Albert Hall concert as part of the Festival and on 19 October the composer conducted his *Don Juan*, *Burleske* and the Sinfonia Domestica. Strauss was, however, present at both the rehearsals and performances by Beecham and the RPO earlier in the month. On 5 October Paul Tortelier was the solo 'cellist in *Don Quixote* and a week later Dennis gave a fine performance in *Ein Heldenleben*, with its divine but very taxing horn solo in the closing bars. One observer said of Dennis, probably thinking of his motoring interests, that when he played the opening bars of *Heldenleben* it looked as if he were changing gear three times! This same concert also featured the Fantasia *Die Frau ohne Schatten*, which Beecham graciously allowed Norman Del Mar to conduct as his London début. The Chelsea Symphony Orchestra concert in November 1946 had impressed Beecham and in June 1947 he had invited Norman to assist him in conducting the RPO. This meant giving up horn-playing and from that date Norman concentrated entirely on conducting. His place in the Philharmonia was taken by Edmund Chapman; Ian Beers became Dennis's second in the RPO and in March 1948 also joined the Philharmonia as third horn.

The Theatre Royal, Drury Lane, had been a regular venue for some of Beecham's RPO concerts for some while. In spring 1947 a series of Mozart concerts had included the K 131 Divertimento which was recorded a short time later. A further series of concerts began with one of works by Mendelssohn to commemorate the centenary of the composer's death: on 2 November Beecham conducted the D minor Piano Concerto and the incidental music to *A Midsummer Night's Dream*. "In the Nocturne," wrote the *Daily Telegraph*, "Mr Brain sounded notes of a rare and lovely mellowness."

Since the early days of the war the Brahms op. 40 Trio for violin, horn and piano had been a regular feature of Dennis's recitals. He had performed it no less than seven times at the National Gallery Concerts with a variety of violinists and pianists, and it was inevitable that, as with so many other works, a recording would be attempted before very long. One unsuccessful attempt was made during the war years with Harry Blech and Denis Matthews. A second attempt followed in late November 1947, again with Denis Matthews but this time with Arthur Grumiaux as violinist. Regrettably this too came to nothing and Dennis never made a successful commercial recording of this most rewarding of chamber works. However, we are fortunate that in May 1974 the BBC finally released a superlative broadcast of the work that Dennis made with Max Salpeter and Cyril Preedy.

On 28 February 1948 Dennis flew to Vienna to give the second public performance, on 3 March with Josef Krips, of Richard Strauss's Second Horn Concerto (the première had been given five years earlier by its dedicatee, Gottfried von Freiburg). As with all the standard repertoire concertos, Dennis played the work without a score. The Second Horn Concerto was composed in 1942, during Strauss's 'Indian Summer', a time when he was living in fear of the Nazis who dominated his war-torn country. It has an extraordinary lightness and clarity of texture. Although the melodies contain some of the chromaticism which characterized his main compositions, there is relatively little that could not be played on the 'natural' E♭ Horn. Even at the age of seventy-eight, Strauss had still recalled what he had learnt from his own father's horn-playing days. Dennis conveyed all these qualities to perfection with the Vienna Symphony Orchestra.

Strauss's Second Horn Concerto joined Britten's Serenade in the small number of solo works that Dennis was able to offer the public. He was aware that the repertoire for the horn had too few modern works of any calibre. Strauss's concerto was a valuable addition but it was still very much in the conventional style; something was needed that would open up new avenues for the performer in the way of technique and interpretation, taking him away from the hunting field and into the realms of contemporary music. One such concerto came from Elisabeth Lutyens. Known chiefly for her smaller-scale instrumental music, she wrote her

Horn Concerto for Dennis as one of a series of chamber concertos. An opportunity for its first performance came at the 1948 International Society for Contemporary Music Holland Festival: Dennis played it in the Kurhaus, Scheveningen, on 12 June with the Residentie Orchestra of the Hague conducted by Fritz Schürmann. It received an enthusiastic welcome from the audience and Elisabeth Lutyens joined Dennis on the platform to share the applause. She was presented with a bunch of red roses by fellow-composer Humphrey Searle: their scent was overpowering, but afterwards Dennis had to admit that while they looked very attractive he could not tell if they had any scent at all! The concerto did not make a deep impression on British audiences. Dennis broadcast the work with the BBC Northern Orchestra in November 1948 and it was not heard more than a couple more times after that.

The 1948 Holland Festival was Dennis's first international festival appearance, and it was closely followed by another. He played Mozart's Third Concerto on 22 and 23 August at the Lucerne Festival, with the Zürich Collegium Musicum and Paul Sacher. It was a busy summer, but the end of the spring season had not been without its moments. On 11 April, after long and difficult negotiations by Walter Legge, Herbert von Karajan made his début with the Philharmonia Orchestra at the Royal Albert Hall. The concert was a mixture of the delightful, featuring Dinu Lipatti as soloist in the Schumann Piano Concerto, the routine (Beethoven's Fifth Symphony) and the near-disastrous—Strauss's *Don Juan* nearly ground to a halt at one point. For all that, the concert began a close association between Karajan and the Philharmonia that was to last over seven years.

If Walter Legge's artistic mind was set at rest, so too was his financial unease, for a while at least. The first three years had not been easy and, pressed in 1947 to obtain a government subsidy for the Philharmonia, Legge stubbornly refused. Help did come, however, from an unexpected quarter. The Maharajah of Mysore wanted to interest himself in the music of the Russian composer, Nicholas Medtner, who was living in exile in London, and saw the Philharmonia as the ideal vehicle. Within a few weeks Legge had flown to Mysore and secured a financial guarantee from the Maharajah, in return for which the Philharmonia undertook to promote and record the works of Medtner. The arrangement was terminated in

1951 because of difficulties in transferring sterling from India to Britain but not before it had helped to put the Philharmonia on a secure footing.

On 19 April Dennis had met Adolf Busch again for the first time in ten years. The Busch Quartet was giving a series of concerts at Chelsea Town Hall and Dennis was invited to play the Mozart K 407 Horn Quintet with them. To say that the performance was with the Busch 'Quartet' is slightly inaccurate: the work is scored for one violin, two violas and 'cello to support the solo horn. For Dennis the occasion was all the more enjoyable because it was Busch who had first brought Dennis before the public, as a seventeen-year-old boy.

Between his summer festival engagements on the continent Dennis took part in an interesting series of concerts at Glyndebourne. The early post-war years had been difficult for this famous opera-house and it was 1950 before Fritz Busch was able to take up his post as musical director. Vittorio Gui conducted two opera series at the Edinburgh Festival in 1948 and 1949, and so that there could still be music at Glyndebourne, Beecham offered to give a series of Mozart concerts with the Royal Philharmonic Orchestra. The offer was glady taken up and four concerts were given on consecutive afternoons from 14 to 17 July. There was a talk in the early afternoon, usually by Beecham himself, or a chamber-music recital, followed, after an interval for tea, by an orchestral concert. Dennis was soloist in two of the four concerts. On 14 July he joined Terence MacDonagh (oboe), Jack Brymer (clarinet) and Gwydion Brooke (bassoon) in the Mozart Sinfonia Concertante K 297b. On the next day he had to go to Guildford to play Mozart's Fourth Concerto with the municipal Philharmonic Orchestra, but he returned to Glyndebourne on the 16th to play Mozart's Second Concerto with the RPO. These concerts, together with a similar group in the spring of 1949, forged a valuable link between the RPO and Glyndebourne, which remained the 'pit' orchestra for all productions there until 1963.

In September 1948 Dennis gave his first Prom and his first Edinburgh Festival performances. At Edinburgh he played the Britten Serenade in the company of old friends, the Boyd Neel Orchestra. The tenor was John Tainsh, a celebrated Edinburgh soloist, who helped to make this concert—the last in a series of ten by the Boyd Neel Orchestra—a memorable one. The continuing popularity of the Serenade and more evidence of Dennis's meteoric rise to success can be found in a notice of this concert in the *Scotsman*:

This is undoubtedly one of Britten's best works and the opportunities it gives to that amazing horn-player, Dennis Brain, are alone worth a great deal. . . . Dennis Brain's horn-playing—so expressive, so finely shaded and always of a brightness which puts it in a different class from the safe but dull German horn-playing—verged on the miraculous.

Five days later Dennis played Mozart's Fourth Horn Concerto at the Proms, with the London Symphony Orchestra conducted by Stanford Robinson. This was the climax of three years of hard work and astounding success. Still only twenty-seven years old, he had an international reputation as soloist, chamber-music player and orchestral musician of more than ordinary abilities. The third generation of the 'Brain Trust' was building fast on the experience and traditions of the first two, and quickly outstripping them.

The Alchemist:
Copper into Gold

On one of his first visits to Germany after the war Dennis bought
a large-bore B♭ single horn from Alexanders in Mainz. He still
favoured the purer tone of his old Raoux instrument too much to
consider abandoning it completely for the German horn. From
time to time, however, he experimented both with the Alexander
and with a B♭ crook, in place of an F, on the Raoux. By the end
of 1948 he was sufficiently convinced of the benefits of the B♭
horn generally to send his Raoux to Paxmans in London to have
it built in that key permanently. They fitted a fixed mouthpipe
in place of the crook, shortened the valve-slides accordingly and
added a thumb-valve to change into A. When the instrument was
returned to Dennis he was horrified: much of the fingering for the
higher notes was completely awry and, as he put it, "It had a roll
on the middle B♭." It had to go back to Paxmans, but as they
also had the Alexander in for alteration Dennis was in somewhat
of a predicament—he was due to play the Strauss First Concerto
at the Royal Albert Hall a couple of days later. In desperation he
tried an 1818 Raoux hand-horn he had bought a year previously
from a colleague. It was a collector's piece: it had a set of Brown
detachable valves and a decorated floral bell, with the date inscribed on it in gold lettering. Dennis admitted later that he had
been a little apprehensive about using it for a solo performance.
The instrument had not been 'blown in' and lacked the 'lining'
which is produced by the combination of breath and dust. Whisky
is an excellent 'liner' but Dennis contented himself with a glass of
orangeade after a performance which betrayed little or nothing
of his own unease. For nearly two years he continued to use the

1818 Raoux with a B♭ crook in preference to his modified Raoux.

During the winter of 1948–9 Aubrey returned to horn-playing. For the moment he did not go back to the BBC Symphony Orchestra; they had appointed Aubrey Thonger principal horn after his illness in 1945 and, in any case, his health would not allow him to undertake any strenuous playing. Dennis arranged for him to play in the Philharmonia as fourth horn from October 1948, and until May 1950 he played fairly regularly with them— usually as fourth or fifth horn, occasionally as second horn, and for a spell in February and March 1950 as sixth horn. His main activity was teaching at the Royal Academy, but his health made even that difficult at times. To make blowing easier he had bought, from a colleague, a second-hand Selmer four-valve horn. Earlier in his career he had completely rejected large-bore horns of any sort, and the change must have been difficult, though it did mean that he could play again.

The flexibility of the London orchestras not only allowed Aubrey to play again fairly readily but for two years had allowed Dennis to enjoy the unique position of principal horn in both the Philharmonia and Royal Philharmonic Orchestras. In the Philharmonia, for example, there were no contracts. Legge had 'first refusal' on the best players and they were paid per session, or per concert and rehearsal. It was no secret that Walter Legge and Sir Thomas Beecham resented players like Dennis 'doubling' in this way, but so long as engagements did not clash the system was workable. Each tried to capture the exclusive loyalty of certain players; Beecham by pushing up the fees of men like Dennis, James Bradshaw and Reginald Kell. A crisis came in December 1948, however, with a proposed tour by the RPO of Bradford, Leeds, Manchester, Hanley and Wolverhampton. The programme included Richard Strauss's *Ein Heldenleben* and the same programme was to be repeated in London in the Royal Albert Hall on 15 December. Dennis's commitments to the Philharmonia prevented him from going on the tour but not from playing in the London concert. Roy White, third horn in the RPO and first horn when Dennis was unavailable, took strong objection to the prospect of playing *Heldenleben*, with its notoriously taxing solos, for the whole tour only to have Dennis return for the London concert. Beecham, who was more easy-going than many might imagine, looked to the broader issues involved and sent for Dennis: he must play for the tour and the London concert or part company with the RPO. Dennis promptly resigned, and for the whole of 1949 Roy White was left as principal horn of the RPO, a year that included Beecham's seventieth Birthday Concert and the Richard Strauss Memorial Concert. Beecham naturally complained. "People come to see *me*," he moaned, "not a clever young horn-player," but even he realized that on this occasion his rivalry with Legge and the Philharmonia had overridden his better judgement.

No sooner had Dennis stepped out of one orchestra than he was into another. On 11 February 1949 he took his place as principal horn of the London Mozart Players for their first concert, in the Wigmore Hall, London. To speak of this occasion as a début would be a half-truth, for the London Mozart Players were a natural extension of Harry Blech's wartime London Wind Players. Stiffness in his shoulders and fingers had drastically reduced Blech's violin-playing, but after the war he had found a new interest in conducting a student orchestra which gave concerts at St Pancras Town Hall. At one of these concerts the pianist Dorothea Braus said to him, "That's how I like to hear Mozart played," and asked him to accompany her in a Mozart concerto. Blech formed a chamber orchestra of some twenty-five to thirty players: they were led by Max Salpeter and many of the wind came from the original London Wind Players.

So were born the London Mozart Players and with them the Haydn-Mozart Society, a non profit-making body which ran the Players. The success of the first Wigmore Hall concert and the second, on 5 April, when Dennis played Mozart's Second Concerto to a packed house, gave Blech sufficient encouragement to abandon his violin and concentrate on conducting full-time with the Players. Three more concerts were given in 1949, one in St Pancras Town Hall and two in the Wigmore Hall, and then for the next eighteen months the Players' regular home was Chelsea Town Hall. From mid-1951 the regular venue for their London concerts became the newly-opened Royal Festival Hall.

Dennis's second in the London Mozart Players was Ian Beers, who had replaced Norman Del Mar in the Royal Philharmonic Orchestra. Del Mar's status as a conductor had grown rapidly since he gave up full-time horn-playing. He continued to direct the concerts given by the Chelsea Symphony Orchestra which, although still amateur, had reached very high standards and brought before the public many rare and interesting works. With Norman Del Mar they achieved a magnificent success by presenting in May 1949 the first London performance of Strauss's Second Horn Concerto, with Dennis as the soloist. The performance had its flaws: the *Daily Express* thought that, while Dennis was 'the inevitable choice for the difficult solo, he was below his best', but the occasional slips were amply compensated by an almost carefree brilliance of execution.

In the same month Karl Haas and the London Baroque Ensemble gave a series of three open-air lunchtime concerts in Russell Square, London. At one of these Dennis and Malcolm Arnold, who was making one of his last appearances as a trumpeter before becoming a full-time composer, played in a series of Cherubini marches for wind instruments. These were made up of short snatches of music, repeated in such a way that thirty seconds of music became a six-minute work. The greatest concentration was needed, but all the players had the utmost difficulty in keeping the music on their stands as a strong wind was blowing! One of the marches threatened to go on forever as both Dennis and Malcolm had lost count of the repeats, but the performance was brought to a merciful close as the wind blew the music right off the stand. The humour of the situation was not lost on either of them—nor was it the only time when they derived hilarity from music-making. Malcolm Arnold once arranged a Hocquet by Guillaume de Machaut for trumpet, horn and trombone, which he and Dennis played together many times and also broadcast for the BBC. They were both so struck by the humour of the piece that they had to stand back-to-back in the studio to avoid breaking into laughter.

In June 1949, Dennis took part in the first of a series of festivals, a Mozart-Beethoven festival in Hastings, organized by the Southern Philharmonic Orchestra whose founder and conductor, Herbert Menges, was a close friend of the Philharmonia. As well as Menges himself, guest conductors for the Festival included Basil Cameron and Sir Thomas Beecham. Dennis arrived to play a Mozart concerto and at the rehearsal confessed to the Orchestra's manager, Morris Smith, that he had cut his lip rather badly while shaving that morning. The cut looked bad and was obviously on the embouchure. Smith was worried that it would affect the performance. Had Dennis tried to see if it would? "Oh no," Dennis replied cheerfully, "but I think it will be quite all right." It was.

At Aix-en-Provence Dennis played Mozart's Third Concerto on 28 July in an all-Mozart concert conducted by Hans Rosbaud. The latter's superlative conducting was the ideal complement to Dennis's artistry, but his playing did not appeal to the French as much as it did to concert-goers in other European countries. Although for British listeners his tone represented the ideal blend of French purity and German roundness, for the French it was too heavy. They preferred a very wide vibrato and an almost saxophone-like silkiness of sound. Earlier in 1949 Dennis and Ian Beers had played in Bach's Brandenburg Concerto no. 1 with the London Baroque Ensemble in the Salle Wagram, Paris, and apart from the occasional Philharmonia concert Dennis only made a couple more appearances in France during his entire career.

Edinburgh was always ready to welcome him, and the 1949 Festival was no exception. The Philharmonia Orchestra gave two concerts with Kubelik, but for Dennis, and the Edinburgh public, the highlight was the concert on the afternoon of 27 August in the Usher Hall. The Busch Quartet had already performed the Brahms and Dvořák Piano Quintets with Rudolf Serkin; now they were joined by Dennis and Frederick Thurston, Paul Draper and James Merrett for the Schubert Octet and the Beethoven Septet. It was a happy collaboration, and all the players were on top form, not least Dennis who, now renowned for his discreet playing in chamber works, inspired the following comment from the *Daily Telegraph*: "Thurston's clarinet was exquisite, and as for Brain, one wondered whether ever before the horn had melted into a chamber ensemble with such faultless tone and subtlety of gradation."

Dennis exploited his rare ability to play in ensembles not just for his own advancement but so as to promote new works for wind instruments. His own Wind Quintet was now well known and was to be found performing works by Ibert, Poulenc and Hindemith, in addition to the classics. One composer in particular had cause to be grateful to Dennis and his Quintet. Peter Racine

Fricker, one of Dennis's old schoolfriends at St Paul's, completed a Wind Quintet in June 1947 and sent a score of it to Dennis, more for his comments than anything else. To his surprise, he opened the *Radio Times* one day to find the work scheduled for a broadcast that week, in January 1949, the first work of his ever to be presented by the BBC. Dennis's kindness to an old schoolfriend did more than give the Quintet a wider public than it might otherwise have had. It won Fricker the Clements Memorial Prize and thus launched him on a successful composing career. Dennis's Quintet played the new work numerous times from then on, both in England and in Europe.

The 1949–50 winter season of London concerts brought some interesting changes in the personnel of the Royal Philharmonic and Philharmonia horn sections. For the Philharmonia's concert on 25 November, when Karajan conducted Beethoven's "Choral" Symphony, Ian Beers moved up to second horn in place of Edmund Chapman. Beers now played second for both the RPO and the Philharmonia, repeating the doubling to which Beecham had objected a year before, losing Dennis from the RPO as a result. This loss had been acutely felt throughout the year and when, in December 1949, Roy White left to return to his native Australia, Beecham took the opportunity to invite Dennis back to his old job. Dennis was pleased to return and for a few concerts early in 1950 he occupied the first horn desk of the RPO. He was, however, too heavily booked for a while to be able to commit himself completely, and so he shared the position with Alan Hyde and Charles Gregory. For four years from October 1950, Dennis played principal horn in both the RPO and the Philharmonia under a uniquely flexible arrangement. The word 'uniquely' is used advisedly: the 1948 *Heldenleben* row had forced Frank Probyn to forsake the Philharmonia for the RPO and by the beginning of May 1950 Ian Beers had been induced to do the same.

For a while Aubrey replaced Ian Beers as second horn in the Philharmonia. It was an ironic reversal of fortunes: ten years before, Dennis had been proud to sit 'next to Dad' in the orchestra. Now Aubrey was only too glad to be able to play second to his son. In fact almost eleven years to the day—on 9 October 1949— after Dennis's Queen's Hall début in Bach's Brandenburg Concerto no. 1, father and son played the same work in a BBC Third Pro-

gramme concert with the Boyd Neel Orchestra conducted by
Nadia Boulanger. They also took part in an important Royal Albert
Hall concert on 22 May 1950 when Furtwängler conducted the
Philharmonia. Kirsten Flagstad gave the first performance of the
Four Last Songs by Richard Strauss. The songs contain some lovely
writing, perhaps one of the finest touches being the little horn
solo at the close of the second song, "September". Of Dennis's
playing the *Musical Quarterly* wrote that it "was as fine as anyone
will ever hear". Unfortunately Aubrey's horn-playing was not so
fine that evening. It showed, particularly in Wagner's "Siegfried's
Journey to the Rhine", that Dennis, out of kindness to his father,
had misguidedly put him in an exposed position which his declining health did not allow him to sustain. Aubrey played second
horn in the Philharmonia only once more, on 25 May. Walter
Legge then told Dennis, kindly but firmly, that his father must
not come back. For the 1950–1 season Neill Sanders was appointed
second horn: he and Dennis, of similar ages and temperaments,
became over the succeeding years a superb duo, as the gramophone
recordings of the period testify. That winter Aubrey went to
Sadler's Wells Opera for a spell as second horn to Livia Gollancz
and then concentrated almost exclusively on teaching. He did
make some more broadcasts, some with Dennis (on 3 July 1950
they played in Telemann's *Tafelmusik* for two horns and strings)
and others by himself (the Ferguson Octet and the Poulenc Sextet
in July 1951, for instance).

Now that Dennis had sorted out his relationship with the Philharmonia and the Royal Philharmonic he began to tailor his other
orchestral commitments to suit his solo playing. He played less
and less for the London Mozart Players, where his place was
eventually taken by Douglas Moore, who had also recently been
appointed first horn in the BBC Symphony Orchestra. Aubrey
Thonger had left the BBC in late 1949 to join the Philharmonia
as fifth horn and 'bumper-up' to Dennis, that is to assist him in
the loud tutti passages of the larger orchestral works and leave
him fresh for the solos. The vacancy in the BBC was advertised,
but not before it had been offered to Dennis. He wrote to them
in December 1949 declining a permanent contract as he felt he
was too young to accept such an appointment! It is more likely
that he felt he had more than enough orchestral work with the

RPO and the Philharmonia without taking on a job which had been his father's pride and joy for so many years and in such an august and revered body as the BBC. He withdrew from the New London Orchestra and Anthony Bernard's London Chamber Orchestra, though he still continued to appear with them as soloist from time to time. Dennis and Gareth Morris had joined the latter orchestra during the war years; even then it was a very fashionable body of players and they all had a warm admiration for Bernard as both conductor and musician. It was also the only orchestra ever from which Dennis and Gareth were sacked. Suddenly, with no warning given, they saw a concert by the London Chamber Orchestra advertised in the *Radio Times* for which they had not been booked. No explanation was ever provided, yet both Dennis and Gareth continued to play many solo engagements for Bernard and the orchestra for several more years and always remained on the best of terms with him.

Dennis's European reputation was rapidly increasing. He made two trips to Germany in the space of six weeks in 1950, to Berlin on 20 April to make some studio recordings for West German Radio and then to Baden-Baden on 8 June to give the first performance of Hindemith's horn concerto. Hindemith had heard Dennis play a Mozart concerto in Baden-Baden the previous year and had been so impressed that he immediately set to work to write a concerto specially for him. It is a remarkable work, evidently written by a man who understood the horn as a player himself, albeit of modest abilities. Dennis treasured a photograph of Hindemith signed by the composer: "from one great horn-player to another". The first movement is stately in character, while the second, although very short, is a gem—a Scherzo of great brilliance, over in a matter of seconds. The Finale is in romantic mood, its cadenza, a setting of a poem (by Hindemith himself) describing the evocative powers of the horn, is written as though it will be sung. On 8 June, Hindemith conducted the first performance in the large Kurhaus Theatre in Baden-Baden: afterwards he gave Dennis a copy of the score inscribed "To the unsurpassed original performer of this work. A grateful composer."

Just one week later, in the Barber Institute, Birmingham, Dennis gave the second performance of yet another new work that had recently come his way. It was a concerto by Gordon Bryan. Based on themes from Scarlatti sonatas, the work had been premièred by Dennis the previous December with Rudolf Schwarz and the Bournemouth Symphony Orchestra. Then, as now in Birmingham, he coupled the new work with a Mozart concerto—no. 3 in E♭. Dennis had two reasons for performing two concertos in one programme: new works were made more palatable to audiences if they were combined with the familiar classics; and in general horn concertos are much shorter than those for piano or violin.

In 1950 Dennis was not only made a Fellow of the Royal Academy of Music but was also awarded the Cobbett Medal of the Worshipful Company of Musicians for his services to chamber music—and it is as well to recall that Dennis was still not thirty years old. From its inception his Wind Quintet had served two ambitions: to widen enthusiasm for wind music generally by presenting high-quality performances of a variety of established classical works; and, by means of these performances, to inspire modern composers to write imaginatively for the medium. Radio listeners had been introduced to such novelties as quintets by Gerhard and Wellesz, Janáček's Mladi Suite and Roussel's Divertimento, and there had been first broadcast performances of quintets by Fricker and Kenneth Essex. There were also two performances of Schoenberg's Quintet in which Dennis directed every bar of the hair-raising music with his eyebrows, the bell of his horn or with his little finger: a quite remarkable achievement. One change had been made to the regular personnel of the Quintet in May 1950 when the bassoonist Tom Wightman emigrated to Australia and was replaced by John Alexandra, Dennis's colleague and principal bassoon in the Philharmonia.

Autumn 1950 brought the Proms and the Edinburgh Festival once more. For the Proms on 17 August Dennis joined Sargent and the BBC Symphony Orchestra to play Mozart's Third Concerto in a "beautifully finished and effortless performance", according to the *Daily Telegraph*. In Edinburgh, life was a little more complicated. With Max Rostal and Franz Osborn he performed what one paper described as 'one of the wonders of the week', the Beethoven op. 17 Horn Sonata and the Brahms Trio. He then had to return to London, much to the regret of the Royal Philharmonic Orchestra who were also in Edinburgh with Beecham, to accompany Glyndebourne Opera in, among other works, a revival of Richard

Strauss's *Ariadne*. Dennis was particularly missed at one of the Sunday afternoon orchestral concerts which Beecham gave between opera series. On 27 August he conducted Haydn's Symphony no. 40 in F, which has a minuet with a very high, taxing horn solo. The critics thought Beecham perverse to omit the movement that afternoon but the truth of the matter was that, without Dennis, he simply could not risk it. The first horn at the time had proved unreliable at a previous concert and Beecham did not want to repeat the disaster in Edinburgh. He was very relieved that Dennis planned to return to the RPO in October on a more permanent basis.

In September, while Dennis again visited Germany, to give the first performance in Berlin of Richard Strauss's Second Concerto, Beecham laid the final plans for a tour of the United States by the RPO. Such a tour had been talked of for over a year, but nobody had really taken the matter seriously until they found that berths had been booked to New York on the *Queen Mary* and that through Columbia Artists no less than fifty-two concerts had been arranged for forty-three cities in sixty-four days! It was the first visit to the USA by a British orchestra since the London Symphony Orchestra went out with Nikisch in 1912: Dennis's father Aubrey had been on that trip so he was naturally keen to go himself on this one. Moreover, Yvonne was able to go with him and make some sort of a holiday out of it. In addition, Dennis, in common with the other principals in the orchestra, would have the opportunity to play concertos and so open up a new avenue for his talents in the USA. Aware of the American attitude to narrow-bore horns, he was faced with the awkward decision as to which instrument to take. He finally took both the Raoux and the Alexander, in a specially built double case which became the curse of the tour as ankles collided with its sharp edges in the aisles of the coaches.

The RPO, with Sir Thomas and Lady Beecham, left Southampton on the *Queen Mary* at 7.00 am on 7 October and after a call at Cherbourg made an uneventful crossing to New York. Uneventful that is except for Yvonne who found even the gentle motion of the *Queen Mary* too much for her digestion and remained in her cabin for most of the voyage. She and Dennis had been paired with Jack Brymer and his wife at table, and the four of them spent a good deal of time together on the whole tour, shopping,

sight-seeing and dining out. They managed to get to the top of the
Empire State Building, but their free time there had already been
earned by a concert on the first day after their arrival. It was in
the Bushnell Auditorium, Hartford, Connecticut, and the success
of the RPO's American début is evident from the following notice
in the *Hartford Times*:

> Beethoven's 8th. . . . His [Beecham's] affection for it with his
> mastery of its texture was splendidly reflected by his 'principals'
> (the British term for first-desk men) especially that brilliant young
> French horn Dennis Brain, Anthony Pini, leader of the 'celli, and
> Gwydion Brook [*sic*], virtuoso of the bassoon.

The early part of the tour was spent 'hopping' up and down the
East Coast from Boston to Washington. Dennis's first solo was in
the Mozart Sinfonia Concertante at the Lyric Theatre, Baltimore,
on 20 October, with Terence MacDonagh, Jack Brymer and
Gwydion Brooke. The tour finally came to rest in New York for
two Carnegie Hall concerts on 27 and 28 October, with a free
day in between. At the second of the concerts Lady Beecham
(Betty Humby) made her one and only solo appearance of the
tour, in Mozart's F major Piano Concerto K 459. Sir Thomas virtually had to prompt her through the entire performance, and for
the remainder of the tour she was 'indisposed'. Various items
were substituted, Mozart's 'Paris' Symphony in Richmond, Vir-
ginia, for instance, and one of the most frequent was the Mozart
Second Horn Concerto, with Dennis as soloist. The first occasion
on which he performed the concerto was on 12 November, at the
second of two concerts the RPO were booked to give in New
Orleans. This was the most southerly part of the tour: after
leaving New York they visited towns in North and South Caro-
lina, Georgia and Alabama. Dennis was scheduled to play a concerto on the tour anyway and had chosen the second Mozart
concerto as it was not only his own favourite but Beecham's too.
Jack Brymer wrote in his diary after the morning rehearsal on the
12th, "How does Dennis do it?" and the following day the *Times-
Picayune* took rather longer to say much the same of the performance itself:

> Lady Beecham was scheduled to appear as soloist in Delius'
> Concerto for Piano and Orchestra but illness prevented her from

coming to New Orleans and a pleasant substitute was made, Mozart's Concerto for Horn and Orchestra, with young Dennis Brain as soloist.

Mozart's music is a field in which Sir Thomas Beecham has long shown special aptitude and this was no disappointment. The score required mostly strings, and they appeared to excellent advantage, Sir Thomas seeming to revel in its light-hearted air. Brain is a very accomplished instrumentalist who played with a pure, mellow tone through the Mozartean intricacies.

From New Orleans, the three coaches transporting the RPO headed north again, now through Tennessee, Kentucky and into Illinois. In Rockford, Illinois, after a concert which had as its encore Massenet's "The Last Sleep of the Virgin", there was a double murder and a suicide outside the Faust Hotel in which the orchestra was staying! The Orchestra Hall, Chicago, had beeen booked for two concerts, on the evening of 25 November and the afternoon of 26 November. Dennis was to play the Mozart no. 2 at the second concert anyway, but he now found that he had to play it for the first as well, again as a substitute for Lady Beecham. According to Jack Brymer, Dennis, playing to a packed house, 'knocked them cold'! Claudia Cassidy, the lively critic of the *Chicago Tribune* expressed her gratitude to Beecham for "the Mozartean grace to give us Dennis Brain's matchless horn-playing and keep it superlative company!"

For Dennis, Chicago was a turning-point in his ideas about the ideal instrument for solo work. He had used his Alexander for some orchestral playing on the tour but had always played the concertos on his Raoux. The purity of his tone had been the quality that had impressed listeners most, but the audience in Chicago's Orchestral Hall contained many horn-players who were not so easily impressed. They indeed admired Dennis's virtuosity and even the purity of his tone; they could not, however, help but be amused by the apparent smallness of his sound compared with that of their own wide-bore horns. After the concert on 25 November they came round to the artists' room asking, admittedly in fun, to see the man who plays the 'gas-pipe'. Dennis took the joke in good part and joined in the general merriment as they all took turns to try, in vain, to get a note out of his instrument; but the remark made a deep impression on him, coming as it did at a time when he was having serious reservations about continuing on a narrow-bore horn.

But Chicago held pleasanter memories. Philip Farkas, one of Chicago's leading horn-players and teachers and now Professor of the Horn at Bloomington University, Indiana, threw a party for Dennis and Yvonne and invited Jack Brymer and his wife as well as many horn-players from the RPO and the Chicago area. Farkas was an agent for Conn, the American horn manufacturers who had offered the RPO horn section free instruments in return for advertising on the tour. At Farkas's house Dennis tried out a 'Stroboconn', a device which tunes by the stroboscopic action of whirling wheels. He was intrigued by it and made several attempts to stop the revolving wheels. After about fifteen minutes trying in vain he shouted "Stop the bloody machine!" and burst out laughing. Farkas was as intrigued as the other players by Dennis's own horn and in particular by his mouthpiece. Dennis offered to get a copy made for him, which he did and sent to Farkas via the conductor Rafael Kubelik. The party was a great success. A buffet supper had been laid out and Yvonne was delighted to see candles on the table: she explained that there had been a shortage at home since the war. With typical American generosity the Farkas rounded up all the candles they could find, together with some rolls of aluminium foil which Yvonne had never seen before. She and Dennis left the house that evening beaming as if they had been given the gifts of the Magi.

The remaining three weeks of the tour took in many towns in the area surrounding Chicago, in the states of Illinois, Wisconsin, Indiana and Michigan. Dennis played the Mozart concerto twice more—in Madison, Wisconsin, on 27 November and in Fort Wayne, Indiana, on 2 December. The K 297b Sinfonia Concertante was also played again, in Lafayette, Indiana, well according to Dennis and the rest, but Leonard, clinging to his privilege as a relative, thought not. There was a third Carnegie Hall concert on 13 December in which Dennis was highlighted in the "Royal Hunt and Storm" from Berlioz's *The Trojans* and which ended with the same composer's *Te Deum*. Bags were packed before a final concert, and then on to the *Queen Mary* and home. Yvonne had her sea legs this time and the voyage passed agreeably and quickly. The waiter who served at the Brains' and Brymers' table had the appropriate name of Jack Payne and knew all about London musicians, including both Dennis and his father: many recollections and anecdotes were exchanged over the meals. They docked at Southampton on Thursday 21 December at the end of a highly successful tour for not only the RPO itself but for its members, among them Dennis. He had added considerably to the reputation he had gained during the 1944 RAF tour and fostered with his records. The misgivings he had felt about his instrument and the choice between narrow and wide bore did not seem so urgent away from the American critics: for a while, at least, he decided to keep the Raoux for solo work. He played mostly on the 1818 Raoux and sent his original Raoux back to Paxmans to have a second rotary valve added, which now put the horn into C alto. This provided very good high notes (A, B, C, D above the stave) and facilitated the low G and pedal G which featured so much in the Schubert Octet. Dennis himself said he preferred the Raoux because a softer and more legato tone was obtainable, partly because of the piston action and partly because of the quality of old, soft metal.

Dennis soon bought himself another car, a brand-new Citroen Light 15 and in the first year he had it travelled 32,000 miles—an indication of the amount of work he undertook outside London. He preferred to travel by car whenever possible, finding it infinitely more relaxing than any other form of transport. He once admitted to Leonard that he was exhausted from spending three consecutive days travelling by train. He also got home as often as he could, even if it meant motoring two hundred miles in between engagements in neighbouring towns, just to spend a few hours with Yvonne. For one Brahms Trio recital in Exeter he drove down for the evening performance and straight back to London on the same night!

No sooner than he was back from America than there began again the busy calendar of performances, concerts and recording sessions. On 22 January 1951 he gave the second performance of Hindemith's concerto, in Cologne with Joseph Keilberth, which was closely followed by a third at the ISCM Festival in Venice. Then, on 7 February in Chelsea Town Hall, he gave the first performance in modern times of Haydn's Concerto no. 1 in D major. In Dennis's own words:

The concerto, though no major work, has much charm and many unusual twists as in the second movement, where the horn, having played the theme in the top octave, is required to jump down two octaves into a register used principally for pedal notes and seldom, if ever, even by contemporary composers, for a melodic phrase.

The concerto was composed in 1762 when Haydn was over-worked and burdened with family troubles. On the last page of the score he got the notation completely mixed up, which prompted him to write later at the bottom of the score, "written while asleep"! The work certainly has no pretensions to genius, but it does possess a charm and gaiety that Dennis was able to convey to perfection. "Dennis Brain", wrote the *Daily Telegraph*, "made the most of his opportunities in a flexible and expressive solo part that will, one hopes, become a regular feature of his repertory."

February 1951 also brought Furtwängler back to Britain to conduct the Philharmonia. All credit is due to Walter Legge for his diplomacy during this period. He managed to stay faithful to his rule of no regular conductor and succeeded in engaging an astonishing array of eminent conductors to work and record with the Philharmonia. Now, in the very same year that Karajan decided to record exclusively for Columbia with the Philharmonia Orchestra, Furtwängler made two visits to London to conduct and record with them. Orchestral concerts and recordings were still the mainstay of the Philharmonia's work but the policy of regular chamber-music concerts continued. In the Kingsway Hall on 26 February Dennis appeared with Jeorg Demus and Arthur Grumiaux in the Brahms Trio. The same hall was the venue for the first London public performance of the Hindemith Horn Concerto, on 16 April. Conducting the Philharmonia for this occasion, which also included the Britten Serenade with Peter Pears, was Norman Del Mar, who had conducted the first broadcast performance of the Hindemith concerto with Dennis as well, on 3 March.

Another composer who admired Dennis's talents was Gordon Jacob. He had first met Dennis during the war when he wrote some music for a documentary film about the RAF and, like Benjamin Britten, was sufficiently impressed not just by his artistry but by his total lack of conceit or pride to write a concerto for him. Jacob frequently consulted Dennis on points of technique, but Dennis's only significant suggestion was that the first move-

Dennis with the newly-rebuilt Raoux instrument at the 1950 Edinburgh Festival. (*photo: Paul Shillabeer*)

Dennis with Hindemith in Baden-Baden for the first performance of Hindemith's Horn Concerto, 8 June 1950. (*photo: Hans-Jürgen Vollrath*)

The Philharmonia's principal wind players in 1951. Dennis Brain is behind with principal trumpet Harold Jackson. The front row (*left to right*) is Sidney Sutcliffe (oboe), Gareth Morris (flute), Cecil James (bassoon) and Frederick Thurston (clarinet). (*photo: Philharmonia photograph*)

The Dennis Brain Trio: Dennis, Wilfred Parry, and Jean Pougnet at Auchinleck House 3 March 1956. (*photo: John McKinnon*)

ment should end with a top C, in spite of a difficult cadenza and many rapid passages immediately preceding it. Dennis gave the first performance with Jacob himself conducting the Riddick String Orchestra on 8 May 1951 in the Wigmore Hall. The concerto quickly became a regular item in Dennis's solo concerts, and in particular one recalls his rapid, woodpecker-like tonguing in the fast-moving Finale. In view of the increasing number of new works Dennis had already brought before the public it is strange to find the *Musical Times* saying of a Mozart performance in April 1952:

> Mr Brain must feel, however, as with several other solo works for his instrument, that the intrinsic musical interest is here secondary to the technical virtuosity required; he might well commission a work to challenge his interpretative as well as his technical skill.

The writer evidently set little store by the Britten Serenade or the Jacob concerto, and it can be argued that, while the Mozart concertos are not of the calibre of his last three symphonies, the Third Concerto at least is susceptible to numerous interpretations.

In May 1951 the first records made by the London Baroque Ensemble, of which Dennis was the original principal horn, came onto the market. They were an immediate success and for over seven years record-buyers were treated to numerous rare works for chamber ensemble as well as first-rate performances of the better-known ones. Karl Haas's enthusiasm had brought about a significant increase in the Ensemble's work and reputation. Haas himself often took part in the concerts: at one he played the mandolin in a Beethoven sonata while Dennis forsook the horn to play the piano accompaniment. On the records Haas conducted even the smallest items, such as the unusual Handel Overture Suite in C for horn and two clarinets (Handel's only use of the clarinet and one of the earliest ever). On the label of the seventy-eight rpm records there was only room to name the "London Baroque Ensemble conducted by Karl Haas", but listeners would surely have liked to know that in works such as the Handel the players were Dennis Brain, Frederick Thurston and Gervase de Peyer. In just over a year some thirty works were issued, in Britain on the Parlophone label and in America on Westminster. Neill Sanders invariably played second horn, as he did with Dennis in the Philharmonia. For works that required more than two horns —the Dvořák D minor Serenade for example—some of Dennis's other colleagues were brought in, among them Ian Beers from the Royal Philharmonic, John Burden from the London Symphony, and the brothers Francis Bradley and Emil Borsdorf.

Dennis still played for the Royal Philharmonic Orchestra as often as he could, most frequently for Beecham or for important recording sessions. In July 1951 he was able to go to Glyndebourne for what was to be Fritz Busch's last season. One of the operas was Mozart's *Così fan Tutte*, with its lovely soprano aria "Per pietà" which contains elaborate horn solos. Dennis just managed to attend the dress rehearsal and after going through "Per pietà" Busch smiled in appreciation. "Do it again, please," he requested, "just for me." At the evening's performance the soprano received the usual clatter of applause. At the conductor's desk Fritz Busch was also applauding—not, however, the figure on the stage but Dennis, who had excelled even the afternoon's rendering.

After a Prom appearance, with Sargent in Mozart's Fourth Concerto, Dennis took Haydn no. 1 to Edinburgh, which he performed in the Freemasons' Hall with Harry Blech and the London Mozart Players on 1 September, in a Festival concert of which the music critic of the *Scotsman* wrote:

> It is difficult to say anything of Dennis Brain's performance, except that he was an alchemist, turning copper into gold. Anyone who plays the horn at all is to be honoured, but when a phenomenon like Brain appears, whose artistic and technical capacities seem limitless, one can only write (like Haydn) 'Laus Deo'.

Dennis unquestionably read reviews like this and could be forgiven for revelling in the kind of notices that most artists would give their right arm to receive. Equally unquestionably, his modest nature made him totally unconcerned by them. He was doing a job that he enjoyed to the full, and his reward was conveying that enjoyment to others. That is not to say he was unaware that he had extraordinary talents: when he heard of a horn-playing friend leaving the profession he agreed it was the best thing he could do. "He's got problems, I'm lucky, I have not," he told a colleague, in utter sincerity and complete modesty.

An event that gave him great pleasure was the West Berlin Festival in September 1951, in which his Wind Quintet was invited to take part. With the German pianist Conrad Hansen they performed quintets by Ibert, Fricker and Milhaud, as well as the Mozart K 452 Piano and Wind Quintet and the Hindemith Horn Sonata. The following day they all went to record the Mozart Quintet for West German Radio in what had been Siemens's private concert-hall in the back of his house. It was a typical September day, and the temperature had suddenly dropped. The piano was tuned to 445 cycles per second and of course Dennis and the others were used to playing at 440: they just could not get up to the correct pitch, especially on such a chilly day. A piano-tuner was standing by, a tiny man who looked rather like Groucho Marx. He produced a bag of tuning-forks and said, "Please choose the one!" They chose and were told "go away". When they returned after half an hour, the piano was beautifully in tune and at the correct pitch. After the German trip the Wind Quintet was joined by Wilfred Parry, who now replaced George Malcolm as their regular pianist and accompanist. George Malcolm had found it increasingly difficult to accommodate all his other musical activities to suit the Quintet's schedules: he nevertheless returned several times later to play with them. Wilfred Parry had been Dennis's personal accompanist for recitals since 1948.

The beginning of the Philharmonia's winter season of concerts in the autumn of 1951 was marked by the first visit of the young Italian conductor, Guido Cantelli, for a series of four concerts in the new Festival Hall. Dennis was away for the first concert but played in the remaining three in programmes that included Brahms's Third Symphony and Wagner's Siegfried Idyll. Both works were soon recorded with the Philharmonia by Cantelli in performances that were outstandingly brilliant. Furtwängler came again on 25 October to conduct them, in Brahms's First Symphony and Beethoven's Fourth Piano Concerto with Myra Hess as the soloist. In the midst of this very busy period Dennis indulged himself by buying another car—a Morris Minor Open Tourer. More significant, however, was his final decision to abandon his Raoux horn in favour of the Alexander wide-bore instrument.

It is an unusual coincidence that during 1951 the columns of the magazine *Music and Letters* had contained a fierce debate on

the various merits and demerits of the French and German instruments. In fact, Dennis's name was mentioned in connection
with his use of the B♭ crook on his Raoux horn, the correspondent
bemoaning the practice as detrimental to the true beauty of tone
obtainable on the narrow-bore instrument. Twenty years previously, Dennis's own father Aubrey had made just the same point,
but even he had turned to the B♭ horn for passages that made
exceptional technical demands upon the player, as in Bach's
Brandenburg Concerto no. 1 for example. Dennis now used the B♭
crook for much the same reason: the increasing demands of the
modern repertoire were such that they required an instrument that
was relatively easy to play in the upper register. Moreover, he
needed a horn that was utterly reliable mechanically and the Raoux
could not stand up much longer to the strain of almost constant
use. Many regretted Dennis's decision to change to the wide-bore
horn, and Dennis himself had some misgivings. He made the
change, however, though with some modifications which helped
to satisfy both his conscience and his critics. Before making the
final break, he sent the Alexander to Paxmans to have a narrower
mouthpipe fitted and the valve-keys angled slightly, so that it
had the 'feel' of the old French horn. He also continued to use the
small mouthpiece that his Uncle Alfred had given him and this,
together with the alterations to the horn itself, produced a sound
which to anyone but the absolute purist was almost indistinguish-
able from that of the Raoux. As on the Raoux, he had extra-strong
springs fitted to the valves to speed up the return action. Paxmans also built an F extension to enable him to obtain the range
of pedal notes missing from the bottom register of the B♭ instrument.

By sticking to a single B♭ horn Dennis satisfied many of the
purists, for he argued, rightly in their view, that while an instrument with a large number of valves provided many convenient
possible changes of fingering the simplest instrument was best for
maintaining purity of tone and accuracy of intonation. He held
that it is the player who produces the sound, whether he plays on
an alphorn or on a suitable length of gas-pipe: provided he uses
his own horn mouthpiece the sound will basically remain the same.
In September 1952 he made his first solo recordings with the Alexander, of Schumann's Adagio and Allegro and Dukas's *Villanelle,*

with Gerald Moore. There is very little difference in tone quality between these recordings and that of the Strauss First Concerto. This is partly the result of studio conditions, which flatter the wide-bore instrument and detract from the narrow, but those who heard Dennis play the works 'in the flesh' admit that while something was lost with the demise of the Raoux it was amply compensated by the artistry that lived on.

✧ 8 ✧

In Top Gear

In May 1952 Karajan took the Philharmonia Orchestra on a three-week tour of Europe—their first. It was to begin in Paris on 12 May and finish in Berlin on 30 May, including Berne, Zürich, Milan and Vienna, a total of sixteen concerts. On the day of the orchestra's first Zürich concert, Walter Legge's wife, the celebrated Elizabeth Schwarzkopf, who was travelling with the tour, bought a huge second-hand Hudson saloon car. It acquired the nickname of the 'Atlantic Liner' and, knowing Dennis's interest in cars, Legge invited him to drive with them to Milan. When they arrived Dennis lost no time in asking if he might have a go at driving the car. Elizabeth agreed, and Dennis enjoyed himself enormously, although at some expense to the other road-users in the city: as he confided to Legge later, "There will be a lot of cyclists in Milan with sore bottoms now, guv'nor!" In Milan, however, Legge was fully occupied with other matters. While still juggling with the rivalries between Karajan and Furtwängler he was contriving to get Toscanini to come to London to conduct the Philharmonia: it would be the maestro's first visit since before the war, when he had conducted the BBC Symphony Orchestra. Legge's ambitions were soon dashed when Toscanini told him that he was too tired to start work with an orchestra that was new to him. Undaunted, Legge arranged that he should hear the broadcast of the Philharmonia's second Milan concert on 20 May, and, as he was packing after the concert to drive back to Zürich that night, the telephone rang. It was Toscanini's daughter: could they come to her father's house at once? There, the maestro came straight to the point. "What programme shall I conduct in London? I am not too tired to conduct *your* orchestra."

Thrilled by the news, Legge was far too tired to drive through the night to Zürich and asked Dennis to take over. The route lay over the Gotthard Pass and when they reached the entrance at dawn they found it officially closed to traffic because of heavy falls of snow. The only alternative was to wait for the first train to take them through the tunnel. Dennis was not content to wait: he insisted that they should drive over the pass. To this day, Legge and his wife, and Gareth Morris, who was in the car with them, recall with awe and delight the cool, expert way in which Dennis handled that enormous car over smooth ice, with ten-foot snowdrifts on one side and sheer drops on the other. As Walter Legge said later, "It was only when driving that Dennis shed his irresponsible, endearing boyishness." The drive, and the Toscanini date, called for some celebration, so later in the tour Legge took the four of them to the best restaurant in Vienna for dinner. After three huge courses of the finest Viennese cuisine Dennis was asked what he would have for dessert. With a perfectly straight face he asked, "I don't suppose they have bread-and-butter pudding?"

After the tour, Dennis was particularly anxious to get back home as Yvonne was expecting their first baby. He did not have long to wait: on 11 June a son, Anthony Paul, was born. After seven years of marriage, the 'fourth generation' (as Dennis nicknamed him) was a welcome addition: many of their friends had young families, and after a long period during which they had been able to enjoy just their own company while they were still young the baby's arrival happily suited their own plans. It did mean that Yvonne would not be able to attend so many of Dennis's concerts or travel quite so much with him, as she liked to do. They were fortunate, however, that her mother was able to baby-sit for them on many occasions. Anthony Paul was duly christened and Gareth Morris was particularly happy to be asked to be a godfather. Dennis lost no time in proudly informing his Uncle Alfred of the new arrival. He wrote:

I will admit that, having seen my wife was alright, the first part of the baby I looked at was his mouth, which looks as though it might bear possibilities.

The birth of a son, however, did not reduce Dennis's own commitments in any way: he was as busy as ever. Just before the European tour, Furtwängler had conducted his last London con-

cert with the Philharmonia: on 24 April Kirsten Flagstad sang
the five *Wesendonck Songs* by Wagner and the closing scene from
Götterdämmerung. Now, in June, Furtwängler made his last, and
greatest recording with them, of *Tristan and Isolde*. The Philharmonia rose nobly to the occasion, amply reinforcing the *Observer's*
description of them as "this well-nigh incredibly perfect orchestra". The following month saw a large block of recording sessions
with Karajan who, by reason of his close association with the
Philharmonia for over four years, could now be regarded as its
principal conductor. The July sessions produced some fine performances of such works as Tchaikovsky's Fifth Symphony,
Sibelius's Fifth Symphony, Brahms's First Symphony, Handel's
Water Music and Sibelius's *Finlandia*, all containing fine horn-
writing. Their passion for cars forged an extra-musical link between Dennis and Karajan: they both knew the specifications of all
the fast cars by heart and never tired of discussing them. Dennis
was the only member of the Philharmonia whom Karajan addressed
by his Christian name, and one of his happiest hours was in
Lucerne in 1954 when Karajan allowed him to drive his Mercedes
300SL. Their relationship is best shown in the story of one recording session at which Dennis fluffed the very first note of a solo.
Quietly Karajan laid his baton on the stand. "Thank God!" he
murmured.

With many years of radio experience behind him, Dennis now
made his first television appearance, on 4 July 1952. It was in a
programme devised to celebrate the reopening of the Goldsmiths'
Hall in London. Between descriptions of the Hall and its furnish-
ings, a variety of artists played selections from well-known pieces
of music. As well as Dennis, the Dutch String Quartet, Max
Gilbert (viola) and Gerald Moore had been invited to take part.
Dennis's own contribution to the programme consisted of Dukas's
Villanelle and the last movement of the Mozart Horn Quintet.

It was perhaps inevitable that August would find Dennis once
more in Edinburgh for the Festival, his fifth successive one. The
Royal Philharmonic Orchestra had a heavy programme of Usher
Hall concerts, in the midst of which Dennis was engaged for two
solo appearances. One was the Brahms Trio, with Josef Szigeti and
Clifford Curzon. The other, a Mozart concerto with the RPO and
John Pritchard, was the climax of three days' travelling and playing

which was typical of the pace at which Dennis was now working. On Sunday 24 August he rehearsed with Pritchard and the RPO in Edinburgh for the following Tuesday's performance of Mozart's Fourth Horn Concerto. The same afternoon, he played for the RPO in Act I of Berlioz's *L'Enfance du Christ*, leaving after the interval (there are no horn parts in Act II) to drive back to London. On Monday morning he rehearsed, and the same evening at the Proms played Mozart's Second Concerto with the London Symphony Orchestra and Stanford Robinson. By 11.00 am on Tuesday he was in the Freemasons' Hall, Edinburgh, for his performance with Pritchard and the RPO! One might expect all this dashing about to take its toll, but the *Daily Telegraph* spoke of 'flawless playing' in the Pritchard concert and the *Scotsman* is worth quoting in full:

How Dennis Brain achieves such a seemingly effortless and relaxed performance is a secret known only to himself. This quality is not necessarily found in all great artists and one would not, for instance, associate it with Szigeti, but when it is present the listener sits back complacently knowing that there is not the remotest possibility of unease. That it might be taken for granted is the only danger. There was no danger of this yesterday . . . no one could fail to appreciate the soloist's feeling for melodic line, the elegance of the phrasing and the unhurried subtlety with which he brought out every little nuance of his part.

This ability to relax was brought home to Jack Brymer the morning of that same concert. He was chatting to Dennis in the wings before he went on to play the concerto about his plans to drive home that afternoon; Dennis was reckoning on reaching Stamford for a pub meal at about 6.00 pm. With the applause still echoing in the hall, Dennis grinned at Jack Brymer as he walked off and said, as if the matter had been running through his mind while he played the concerto, "Perhaps Grantham would be better."

All through September 1952 plans went ahead for the Toscanini concerts with the Philharmonia Orchestra. They were to be given in the Royal Festival Hall on 29 September and 1 October and the programmes had been agreed; all the Brahms Symphonies, his Tragic Overture and the Haydn Variations. That over sixty thousand people applied for just seven thousand seats reflects the excitement with which the concerts were awaited: they promised to be the musical climax of the year, if not the decade. Nobody who heard them will forget the way the Philharmonia gave of their superb best. Every member was afraid to play less than perfectly, and with a group so keyed up one could easily forgive the trombonist who, after an interminable wait with no chance to 'warm up', muffed the chorale in the First Symphony, and the violinist who was so eager to come in on time that he came in two bars early. After the second concert, a heart-melting Third Symphony and a glorious Fourth which even the fireworks let off by hooligans at the back of the hall could not spoil, four players were summoned backstage to the maestro's dressing-room. Dennis was one of them, as was Gareth Morris, and they both later commented on the great man's kindly humanity: the way he had smiled as the leader, Manoug Parikian, had held him from falling on the rostrum steps and when the oboist had played a particularly beautiful solo. Dennis described it as a "sweet smile, almost countrified", but it was nothing to the smile that Toscanini had for Dennis himself, who had excelled even his own virtuosity by playing all the famous solos with a golden radiance. Neville Cardus summed up his playing particularly well:

> It is pretty certain that Toscanini, as much as the audience, admired the horn-playing of Dennis Brain. The solo in the finale of the C minor came forth like sun from the mists; it was beautifully intoned out of a sort of wrought gold of music. And at the end of the first movement of the second symphony he breathed a whole tradition of romance into his instrument; the fall of the cadence touched the heart more than anything else in the concert.

The remainder of October was very busy for the Philharmonia, with a group of four more concerts with Cantelli. For those on 21 and 23 October Aubrey returned to play seventh horn. Though he was well enough in himself, he was finding it increasingly difficult to move about. He had to use sticks most of the time and Dennis had to help him on and off the concert platform and carry his instrument for him.

Now that they had a family, Dennis and Yvonne had been looking for a larger house. The bungalow at Hayes was really too small and since Dennis was no longer in the RAF they wanted to live somewhere more central. They found a large, detached house in Frognal, Hampstead, which they took to at once: it had a charming horn motif engraved on the living-room fireplace. The house was large—too large for the furniture they had at Hayes—but the prospect of the new surroundings was exciting. They moved on 8 December, right in the middle of the great London 'smog'. Very soon the house acquired the elegance that their position undoubtedly deserved, but it also had a homely atmosphere which they gladly shared with their friends. Soon after they moved Dennis bought another car, one of the very few 1939 12-cylinder Lagondas. It had a short life, however. On the way to a Wind Quintet concert in Bangor he hit a lorry just outside Dunstable, on the A5. Stephen Waters, the Quintet's clarinettist, was in the car with Dennis and although they were both severely shaken neither was badly hurt. They were taken to the local hospital for a check-up and soon had to abandon any attempts to reach Bangor. Leonard and the others had to make the best of things: a couple of trios were found by the University's music department, which also supplied some string players for larger-scale works. Dennis had to write off the Lagonda: such was its sturdiness that it had not only protected its passengers from serious injury but had succeeded in knocking the lorry off the road into a field. After that it was too badly damaged to consider repairing. Dennis never had time to tinker with his cars beyond simple repairs or changing the oil or the plugs. He replaced the Lagonda with another Citroen, a 1938 model which had once belonged to the cellist Boris Rikelman. Not long after, he sold it to Leonard and bought a 6-cylinder Citroen which he used for the rest of his life.

Dennis visited Germany in May 1953 and made a number of recordings for Berlin Radio and South-West German Radio. He was booked to do his first concert in Mainz but was unable to clear his instrument through Customs in time. He called into Alexanders, bought another horn from them and played it that same evening—something very few players would do on any instrument. Dennis frequently visited Alexanders and worked closely with them in promoting the five-valve horn and the F alto horn. During the summer of 1953 he tried out a five-valve horn: it was pitched in B♭ and A as before but with an ascending D valve in addition, which gave a very wide range. He was never happy with

it and soon went back to his original Alexander B♭. An F alto
horn which he had bought at about the same time he never used,
and in 1954 he sold it to Alfred Cursue, his colleague in the Philharmonia. On another occasion Dennis called into Alexanders with
his instrument, saying that there were difficulties with the air
passing. On examination a wooden clothes-peg was found to be
lodged in the bell!

While he was in Germany his fame spread to an unexpected
area of the world. On the famous British-led expedition to Mount
Everest *The Times*'s correspondent, James Morris, had taken out
a supply of gramophone records. Among them were Dennis's
records of Mozart's Second and Fourth Horn Concertos, and
Morris played them to the Sherpas, who listened with evident
delight. The news of the ascent of Everest reached London just
in time for the coronation. Dennis was involved not just in the
many concerts leading up to the ceremony on 2 June but also
in the events in Westminster Abbey on the day itself. For the
service a special orchestra had been assembled from the leading
players in most of the British orchestras. Dennis led the horn
section and with him were John Burden (London Symphony),
Sidney Coulston (BBC Northern) and Charles Gregory (London
Philharmonic).

The summer was never a time when Dennis could afford to take
things easy or plan a long holiday. He and Yvonne had to snatch
the occasional days away when they could, which was not very
often, or use tours like the Royal Philharmonic's visit to the USA
as a holiday. In fact, the summer was fast becoming the busiest
time of all, as it was then that most of the major European festivals
took place. The year 1953 was no exception. At Aldeburgh, in
June, Dennis gave a dazzling performance of the Haydn First
Concerto. Works like this and the Mozart Quintet, for example,
were now being taken seriously by the public, along with the
Mozart and Strauss concertos, for here at last was a performer
who could bring them alive and give them a sparkle and excitement that was almost part of the process of composition itself.
At the Haydn performance Dennis was brought back onto the platform five times to acknowledge the roaring applause and he sat
down to play the last movement again. The encore was as rousing
as before—this for a work that London had not heard of in 1950

and which the composer himself confessed he had written "while asleep". In August he went to Edinburgh, but for the first time merely as an orchestral player, at his customary desk in the Philharmonia for three concerts with Karajan and one with Boult. The press did not allow him to remain unnoticed. Of the slow movement of Tchaikovsky's Fifth Symphony the *Daily Telegraph* said: "As for the famous solo, it may be that never before has it been so beautifully played. Mr Brain maintained it at an almost unbelievably soft level, with infallible control."

On the afternoon of 14 June 1953 the London Baroque Orchestra made its public début at the Royal Festival Hall. Led by Thomas Carter, it was an extension of Karl Haas's Ensemble, enabling him to play slightly more substantial works (though it still only numbered twenty-eight players in all). This first programme was a miscellany of rare and unusual items ranging from the Schubert Konzertstück in D for violin and orchestra to six of the Beethoven Minuets. Dennis was in his usual place as first horn, but next to him was his father, making his only appearance with the London Baroque players. He was deputizing for Edmund Chapman who had been originally booked as second and was unable to play at the last moment. This was one of Aubrey's last public London appearances. Dennis was back in the Festival Hall the same evening, in the Recital Room, to play the Mozart Quintet K 407 with the Martin String Quartet. As in the Haydn concerto he had played at Aldeburgh, he projected his personality through music that many thought was not highly inspired and gave it new life. The Mozart Quintet was in the words of the *Daily Telegraph* again, 'not a major work, but one delightful to hear especially when Dennis Brain takes part'.

In the recording studios it was a particularly busy year for the Philharmonia. Most of the recordings were with Karajan. Some of June and most of July was taken up with Kingsway Hall sessions; Strauss's Four Last Songs were recorded in Watford Town Hall with Elizabeth Schwarzkopf and Otto Ackermann in September, and then Kingsway Hall was booked for 10–13 November for Beethoven's Second and Fourth Symphonies with Karajan. In between these Beethoven sessions Dennis put onto LP all the four Mozart horn concertos. They were, as the gramophone journals quickly pointed out, long overdue: only two of them had been recorded by Dennis before, and these were both on 78s dating from the mid-1940s. Popular as these earlier records had been, even the most optimistic prophets could not have envisaged the success that the new LP enjoyed. Within a very few years it had sold over a hundred thousand copies, a very high number indeed for a record selling at the top price level. It was issued in October 1954 and for nearly twenty years maintained a place in EMI's 'top 20' selling bracket, alongside such old warhorses as the Tchaikovsky B♭ minor Piano Concerto. The recording brought the concertos from comparative obscurity to the forefront of popularity—in particular, the last movement of the Fourth Mozart Concerto is now perhaps as widely known among the general public as any piece of classical music.

The 'takes' of the Mozart concertos went smoothly, but one point in a movement puzzled Karajan. He made his way over to the separate podium where Dennis was placed, his index finger ready to point out the place on the solo part. What he found on the stand, however, was the latest issue of *Autocar*, which Dennis was studying intently! Dennis hardly ever attended a recording session, rehearsal or even a concert without one or more motoring magazines in which he would bury himself during breaks and often while counting long rests. It became a standing joke in the Philharmonia: it was also a mark of his highly individualistic personality which endeared him to his colleagues. Always arriving punctually, though at the last minute, racing out first to the canteen, he brought a constant sense of enjoyment to those around him. He also unnerved unsuspecting conductors, audiences and colleagues alike by his habit of waiting to play a solo passage with complete detachment: then, only seconds before he had to play, he would lift the horn straight to his lips, without so much as a glance at the ogling conductor. It was an outward symbol of his inward calmness. A famous neurologist once told Frank Probyn that Dennis had the perfect, balanced nervous system. His remarkable equanimity took the tension out of any situation. He professed to have no nerves although just one or two pieces did give him some worries. He had no time to practise at home, but as he did some casual warming-up before an Ensemble concert he could often be heard trying over the end of the Poulenc Sextet, which is exceedingly difficult. The only orchestral solo that caused him any alarm was the slow movement of the Beethoven Second Symphony. He would often joke with Sidney Coulston, principal horn of the BBC Northern Orchestra, that he was going to split it one day: sure enough, late one night Coulston's telephone rang. "It's Dennis here. I've split it."

In the intervals of the recording sessions the whole horn section would dash across the road to their favourite restaurant. Dennis could get through a whole dish of spaghetti without the slightest effect on his playing, while a cup of tea and a sandwich wrought havoc on the embouchures of the other horns. Dennis's love of good food was also legendary: he could manage two helpings of most things, but, while it is true that he had to diet at one stage because of overweight, he only had what one could describe as a 'good, healthy' appetite.

Dennis's catholic musical taste and experience manifested itself in a number of ways. A fine organist, he played at the weddings of many of his friends—indeed, he often said he preferred the organ to the horn and regretted that he had so little time to play. Walter Legge realized this, and with the intention of pleasing Dennis and amusing Karajan got him to play the organ on one of the Philharmonia's recordings, in the Intermezzo from *Cavalleria Rusticana*. He sought occasional relaxation through jazz: occasional, because time did not allow many opportunities and he also maintained that the trombone was better suited to that kind of playing. Nevertheless, in addition to his wartime appearances with Geraldo, he also broadcast with Ted Heath and his Band on "Downbeat" in November 1949, playing Duke Ellington's "Sophisticated Lady". Much later, Dennis also recorded two waltzes with Bob Sharples and his Orchestra, for Decca. Sharples' sleeve-note for the first of these, "Will You Remember", is worth quoting, not only for its tribute to Dennis, but for the rather quaint phraseology of the last few words:

An immaculate performance from Dennis Brain who for my money is the best horn-player in the world. At the end he goes up to an almost unobtainable note on the horn and holds it beautifully whilst I resolve the orchestra around him.

The winter of 1953–4 was busier than ever with solo work. Out of the Royal Philharmonic Orchestra had sprung the Wigmore

Ensemble, which gave occasional concerts of chamber-music. On 8 December there was a Festival Hall concert at which they played the Poulenc Sextet and Dix-sept Variations by Damase for wind quintet; Dennis also played the Dukas *Villanelle*. Harry Blech's London Wind Players appeared again in February 1954 when they repeated their 1942 inaugural programme of Mozart's Divertimento in B♭ K 361, and Dennis, although officially no longer with them, returned to lead the horns. A poignant performance was that on 16 February when Dennis and Leon Goossens joined the Jacques Orchestra for Bach's B minor Mass in memory of Kathleen Ferrier, who had died the previous October. Only two and a half years previously they had all performed the same work with her in the Festival Hall. On a more nostalgic note, Gareth Morris achieved the near-impossible feat of gathering together thirty-five ex-RAF Orchestra musicians for a dinner at the International Music Association Club on 2 March to honour their old conductor, R. P. O'Donnell. As well as Dennis and his brother Leonard, John Hollingsworth, Denis Matthews, Harry Blech, Norman Del Mar, Harvey Phillips, Leonard Hirsch and Howard Ferguson were all present. It was a pleasant evening's relaxation in the middle of a very busy period.

On 28 March Dennis helped to introduce an interesting new work to London audiences. At the Victoria and Albert Museum, with Colin Horsley and Manoug Parikian, he gave the first performance of Lennox Berkeley's Trio for violin, horn and piano. Written for the same combination of instruments as the Brahms Trio op. 40, the new work had been commissioned by Colin Horsley because he had so much enjoyed playing the Brahms work with Dennis. Horsley was even more impressed when they met to rehearse the Berkeley Trio by Dennis's quick and perceptive understanding of the new work. The programme that day also included the Mozart K 452 Piano and Wind Quintet, and the following day both works were recorded for HMV. Dennis had renamed his Quintet the Dennis Brain Wind Ensemble, as it frequently appeared in smaller or larger groups for specific works. Cecil James had now replaced John Alexandra as the Ensemble's bassoonist.

Dennis made his last appearance as principal horn of the Royal Philharmonic Orchestra on 7 April, thus ending the unique

The Hoffnung
Festival Concert,
13 November 1956
in the Royal
Festival Hall.
Dennis performs
Leopold Mozart's
Alphorn Concerto
on a hosepipe.
(*photo: Rob
Melville*)

The last photo.
Dennis chats
to Eugene
Ormandy at
Edinburgh,
Saturday 31
August 1957.
(*photo: Hans
Geiger*)

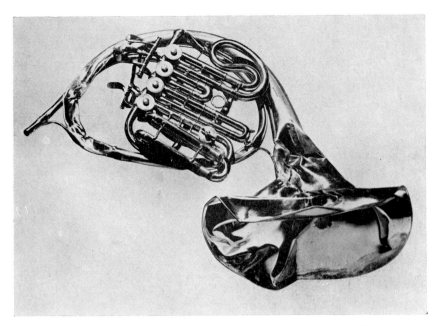

A labour of love. Dennis's instrument as it was damaged in his fatal car accident (*above*) and after re-construction by Paxman Brothers of London (*below*). (*photos: Paxman Brothers*)

arrangement which had enabled him to double with the Philharmonia. Ever since the USA tour in 1950 he had played as regularly as he could for the RPO, more often than not for Beecham, though he always gave the Philharmonia priority when there was a clash of dates. By early 1953 he was finding it more and more difficult to fill both posts. Alan Civil, who had joined the RPO in 1952 as third horn, helped out by doubling as first with Dennis for much of 1953, but by the end of the year even this arrangement was stretched to the limit. Dennis left the RPO and Alan Civil took over as its permanent first horn.

On 6 April Dennis took part in an interesting Festival Hall concert which was both presented and broadcast by the BBC's Third Programme. It was an exact replica of Schubert's only public recital given on 26 March 1828, and comprised recitals of Lieder, choruses, the E♭ Piano Trio and the String Quartet in G. The artists taking part included the New London Quartet, the BBC Men's Chorus, the Robert Masters Piano Trio and the tenor Richard Lewis. His accompanist was Ernest Lush and for one of the songs, the lovely "Auf dem Strom", they were joined by Dennis, who played the very taxing horn obbligato. It was not only one of the highlights of the evening but, as can be heard from a recording which still exists, a performance of unique and inspired musicianship.

Dennis continued to bring new works before the public. He had a disarming way of approaching almost every composer he met and asking him to write a concerto. Most of them willingly obliged—in fact few of them needed to be asked, and Dennis gave each new work a fair trial and the benefit of his adventurous enthusiasm, even if the work did not merit more than a couple of performances. Some which made only brief appearances were the Frank Martin Concerto for seven wind instruments, percussion and orchestra, first performed on the Third Programme in March 1951, the York Bowen Ballade for oboe, horn and piano, in March 1952, and the Concertino by Maurice Blower, which was first heard in Petersfield during the Festival of Britain and in London in July 1953. When Dennis gave the first London performance of the Sonatina for horn and piano by Hans Schreiter at Kenwood Orangery on 27 June 1954 the *Daily Telegraph* commented that "Mr Brain's mellow tone could not ameliorate the ugliness of the new works".

New works require new media for expression. Dennis's own Ensemble was a versatile group in this respect and could offer numerous permutations of instruments. The programme for the Kenwood concert, which incidentally they had given the previous day at the York Festival, is a typical example: Mozart's Quintet for Wind K 270, his Piano and Wind Quintet K 452, Milhaud's Trio for Wind, the Schreiter Sonatina and Fricker's Wind Quintet. After a trip to Germany in early May, Dennis had formed the Dennis Brain Trio, as a fresh outlet for his talents. This combination offered violin or horn sonatas as well as the trios by Brahms and Berkeley, both of which Dennis enjoyed immensely but, since there was no violinist, could not include in his Ensemble's concerts. For his Trio he chose Wilfred Parry as his accompanist; the violinist was Jean Pougnet, a man whom Dennis greatly admired. They had met as a trio once before, at a South Place Sunday Concert in November 1952, to play the Brahms Trio. Only one concert was given at the outset, on 22 May at Painswick in Gloucestershire, and over eighteen months were to pass before there was time for them to team up again on a regular basis.

The Philharmonia Orchestra was booked for no less than three festivals in the summer of 1954, at Aix-en-Provence, Lucerne and Edinburgh. Only two concerts were played at Aix-en-Provence, both with Karajan, on 28 and 30 July. On the 29th Dennis was met by Colin Horsley and Max Rostal for a chamber-music recital given in the courtyard of the Archbishop's palace (open to the air, as was a complete little opera house). They played the Brahms and Berkeley Trios and, though it could be almost guaranteed not to rain in July, that evening the wind blew and the music had to be held on the stands with clothes-pegs. Dennis was then with the Philharmonia in Lucerne for nearly three weeks. Karajan only conducted two of the nine concerts, the remainder being shared among Kubelik, Fricsay, Fischer, Clutyens and Furtwängler. This was to be the Philharmonia's last meeting with Furtwängler: the following November he was dead. Yvonne joined Dennis in Lucerne with Tony, now just two years old, and the three of them enjoyed something of a holiday. Dennis and Yvonne were very fond of Lucerne, so much so that it was almost a second home to them.

The Philharmonia were not due in Edinburgh until 6 September, for three concerts with Karajan and three with Cantelli, but Dennis was booked for two solo appearances on the 1st and the 3rd. On the 1st he brought the Hindemith concerto to Edinburgh audiences for the first time. The Usher Hall was not as full as usual, a pity in view of the interest of the programme. No praise was stinted for Dennis's playing nor, on the whole, for that of the Hamburg Radio Orchestra and its conductor Hans Schmidt-Isserstedt, but the critics were less warm in their reception of the concerto. They complained that even Dennis could not "defend the absurd poem which the horn is supposed to recite in the last movement". To be fair, these remarks must be set against their demands that the work should be heard again in Edinburgh at the earliest opportunity. The Concerto for Horn and Strings by the Swiss composer Othmar Schoek got a similar welcome two days later when Dennis gave its first British performance in the Freemasons' Hall with the Zürich Collegium Musicum. The *Scotsman* called it "tuneful, unpretentious" and commented that Dennis Brain was "admirable as ever, though here his virtuosity was not tested to its limits".

Dennis had a great affection for the Hindemith Concerto. In August 1951 he had written to Alec Robertson, the BBC's head of music talks, "I am glad you like the Hindemith, it is a most interesting and musical work instead of the more usual virtuoso piece." Perhaps with the intention of making it known to a wider audience he approached Walter Legge about recording it, if possible with Klemperer, who had just signed a contract with Columbia. The chance came during Klemperer's first Kingsway Hall sessions in early October 1954, and on the morning of the 7th they began work on the piece. From the first 'take' it was evident that there were difficulties: Klemperer's conception of the tempo was clearly much slower than Dennis's who, denied the fluency he required, had to take unmusical breaths and make obvious breaks in the phrasing. Tension grew and Dennis, feeling deprived of the chance to do justice to both the concerto and himself, went to see Walter Legge. Unless Klemperer was prepared to be more accommodating, Dennis said that he could not continue with something that would obviously not be published. The session continued, but tension did not ease. Dennis, who never lost his temper with anyone, simply grew quieter and quieter until, after a session spent on an orchestral passage, a search revealed that he had packed up his instrument and slipped away! Legge was faced with an awful dilemma and all credit is due to him for the way he handled the situation. He changed the programme for the evening session to another Hindemith work—the Nobilissima Visione Suite, and Dennis agreed to come to the rehearsal and behave as if nothing had happened. Mutual respect and harmonious relations were thus restored. Dennis was able to record the concerto two years later in a much more happy collaboration, with the composer himself.

Klemperer was the only conductor with whom Dennis did not get on well: his temperament was too German for Dennis's adaptable personality, and he always complained that Dennis's playing of the solo in the last movement of Brahms's First Symphony was not strong enough. He also objected to Dennis's habit of reading during rehearsals and once demanded "Mr Brain, you will kindly not read French novels during my rehearsals!", to which Dennis replied, "Dr Klemperer, I shall read what I like." A trifling incident perhaps, but indicative that despite their differences the two of them had a mutual, if cool, respect for each other. At any rate, the remaining sessions went smoothly enough with excellent recordings of the Brahms Haydn Variations and Mozart's Symphonies nos. 29 and 41. At one rehearsal of the former Symphony Dennis was heard quietly, but absolutely accurately, joining the strings in the rapid staccato scales in the last movement.

A Wigmore Hall concert was planned for 4 December 1954 in memory of Noel Mewton-Wood, the pianist who had tragically committed suicide earlier in the year. Works were written specially for the occasion by Alan Bush and Arthur Bliss, and it was particularly appropriate that Benjamin Britten should also write a new work as a tribute, since Mewton-Wood had been a regular performer at the Aldeburgh Festival and had frequently appeared with both Dennis and Peter Pears, for whom the work was composed. It was a canticle for tenor, horn and strings, based on the poem "Still Falls the Rain" by Edith Sitwell. The canticle was a form Britten had derived from Purcell's extended vocal works. The poem is a meditation on the London air-raids, and, while the combination of voice and instrument recalls the Serenade, it was a mature, if less vividly coloured work. The concert had to be postponed because of the illness of Peter Pears, but on 28 January 1955 Dennis gave the first performance of the Britten canticle, as well as two new works by Alan Bush for horn and piano, "Autumn Poem" and "Trent's Broad Reaches".

Dennis revisited Edinburgh twice during winter 1954–5. On the first occasion, 18 November 1954, he played the Britten Serenade and the Gordon Jacob concerto with the University's Reid Orchestra, conducted by Sidney Newman. As usual he stayed with a friend, Graham Melville-Mason. They both loved good food and one of their regular calls was to the Beehive Restaurant in the Grassmarket. On free afternoons Dennis would invariably visit the Écurie Écosse headquarters in Bruntsfield. On this particular occasion there was some time to spare between the morning rehearsal and lunch. As the Anatomy Museum of the Medical School was nearby, Mason took Dennis for a look round. Dennis was fascinated by the exhibits, scientific, historical and horrific, and in particular by the glass jars showing the various stages of development of the human foetus. As they left the Museum he spotted one of the notices giving lists of operations due to take place in the Royal Infirmary and was amused that they should be displayed like theatre-bills. Told that medical students could go in and watch anything that interested them, his eyes lit up and he begged Mason to take him to see an operation in progress. There was no time then, but on 21 January he was due back in Edinburgh to play Mozart's Third Concerto and the Britten Serenade again, with Karl Rankl and the Scottish National Orchestra. Sure enough, a few days before, Mason received a letter from Dennis to say he would arrive first thing on the 21st and hoped he had not forgotten the operation. Mason had not forgotten and Dennis was duly masked and gowned by a helpful nurse and told to 'hover' at the back until he felt he could bring himself to watch. In a few moments Dennis was by the table, engrossed in the gastrectomy being performed by a Mr Adamson. After it was over Mason reminded him of their 'Beehive' lunch prior to the afternoon's rehearsal. "That can wait, Graham," Dennis retorted, totally absorbed. "What's on next here?" They stayed on, leaving time enough only for a quick snack before the rehearsal. The crowning moment was Dennis's description of the morning's entertainment to Peter Pears in the artists' room—Pears turned greener and greener as the description became more graphic.

Dennis did a great deal of travelling during the early months of 1955. As well as Edinburgh and Glasgow appearances with the Scottish National Orchestra, he visited Liverpool to play Strauss's Second Concerto and Hull, Keighley and Leeds with the Yorkshire Symphony Orchestra—all in the space of a fortnight. In addition to the Britten Serenade and concertos such as that by Gordon Jacob, he still regularly played all the Mozart concertos, particularly his favourite, no. 2. Although he may have irked at the limitations of the repertoire he allowed nothing to mar the freshness of his playing. Of a March performance of the Mozart Second Concerto *The Times* commented,

> He played in Mozart's second Horn Concerto and played it first as though he had just discovered it, and secondly as though his instrument were a supremely agile human voice, not a machine dependent on pistons and on harmonic series.

Dennis's playing always had a creative quality. Mozart might have written the concertos with him in mind, such was the dimension added by his performances of them.

Peter Racine Fricker wrote a Sonata for Horn and Piano for Dennis between January and March 1955 and Dennis gave its first performance with Harry Isaacs at a South Place concert on 20 March in the Conway Hall. Exactly one month later he broadcast in the Third Programme a concerto by Kenneth Essex: encouraged by Dennis's performance, Essex wrote to the BBC to ask them to consider the work for inclusion in that summer's Prom concerts, but the BBC instead chose the Seiber Notturno. In early June Dennis went to Berlin to perform the Danzi horn concerto and then returned to prepare both himself and his Ensemble for two appearances at the Aldeburgh Festival. Peter Pears and Benjamin Britten had commissioned Humphrey Searle to write a new work for Dennis to play there and on 21 June he performed the Aubade for horn and strings, with Walter Goehr and the Festival Orchestra. The work bore the dedication 'For Dennis Brain and the Aldeburgh Festival 1955'. In the same programme Dennis included Haydn's Second Concerto in D, a work which he played very rarely. It contains wide leaps to pedal notes, which he did not find easy and which, it will be remembered, his Uncle Alfred had found equally difficult. On the following day, the Ensemble played Beethoven's Piano and Wind Quintet op. 16, in Aldeburgh's parish church with Britten at the piano. Dennis and Peter Pears performed the Canticle "Still Falls the Rain", and there were also wind quintets by Mozart and Milhaud.

On 23 July Dennis broadcast a talk entitled 'The Early Horn'. Lecture-recitals had for some time been a small part of his work: his natural shyness kept him from giving many talks, though he did visit quite a number of schools. As early as 1950 he had been approached by Alec Robertson to take part in the programme "To speak for Myself" but had demurred, asking for time to consider the idea more fully. Nothing more came of it, but on 1 February he gave a lecture-recital in the Royal Festival Hall which included Mozart's First Concerto (with piano accompaniment), the Beethoven and York Bowen Sonatas and the Dukas *Villanelle*. With his colleagues from the Philharmonia Orchestra, he also gave the first performance in England of Hindemith's Sonata for four horns, which Hindemith had written for the horn-players of the Vienna Symphony Orchestra in 1953. Roger Fiske of the BBC heard the talk and suggested that Dennis did something similar for a broadcast as soon as possible. Dennis showed more interest this time, and Fiske contacted Reginald Morley-Pegge, the expert on the early horn and its music, for some ideas. Morley-Pegge had the parts for Keiser's opera *Octavia*—the first truly *orchestral* horn parts—and in addition suggested excerpts from Handel's L'Allegro and the *Water Music*, as well as Schubert's "Auf dem Strom". Dennis in fact used these last two items (with a soprano rather than tenor for the Schubert song) as well as a Bach Cantata, and in addition to concertos by Vivaldi and Rosetti, Dennis also gave the first performance of the Mozart Fragment in E. At one time thought to be the missing middle movement of the K 412 concerto, the piece has obvious first-movement characteristics, and Dennis lamented that only about a dozen bars remain of what promised to be one of Mozart's finest wind concertos. Dennis had now played all the Mozart works for horn except the unfinished Concerto Rondo in E♭. Alan Civil had been given a copy of the horn part by Aubrey during the war and when Dennis mentioned one day that he had never played the piece, Civil decided to try to finish it in order to give him an ideal encore to follow the concertos. He did not accomplish it in time, however.

The day after the BBC talk, Dennis flew with the rest of the Philharmonia to Vienna to spend five days recording Beethoven's "Choral" Symphony with Karajan and the Singverein of the Vienna Gesellschaft der Musikfreunde. This was one of the very first recordings to be made in stereo, although it was never issued in that form. As was usual practice, Dennis played the famous solo for the fourth horn in the slow movement himself. Nobody ever begrudged him this—in fact everyone was more than happy to leave it to him. Dennis never aroused any jealousy among his colleagues: the best of them were only too pleased to play along- side him. He had to leave the Vienna sessions early to return to London for his Prom performance of Seiber's Notturno. Although the work was being heard for the first time by a Prom audience it had long been a regular feature of Dennis's concerts. Seiber had written it for him (the dedication was to the memory of Brahms) and Dennis had given it its première in December 1945 at the Wigmore Hall. The Prom performance was highly satisfactory: the composer himself was present and came round to the artists' room afterwards to thank Dennis. There was a second Prom on 7 September, which included the Mozart Second Concerto and the Britten Serenade, in which, according to one paper, Dennis seemed worried by problems of balance—a rare criticism.

On Saturday 17 September 1955 Aubrey had a serious fall and as a result suffered a heart attack. He was rushed to hospital and for a day or two seemed to be making good progress but died on Tuesday 20 September, aged sixty-two. His death caused considerably less stir than it might have done thirty years earlier. He had given up performing in public and for the last two years had confined his activities almost entirely to teaching: one of his last appearances had been at the Canford Summer School in mid-August. For a man who had at one time been unrivalled in his field the events of the post-war years were a sad epilogue. Attempts to return to orchestral playing brought little satisfac- tion and were almost entirely a result of Dennis's well-inten- tioned, if perhaps misguided, consideration. His failing health preyed on his nerves and affected his behaviour towards his col- leagues from time to time. At rehearsals he would say, "Do you remember this piece that always gave us so much trouble?" and then proceed to play it very badly, when in his younger days he could have managed it without the slightest bother. In his calmer moments he tried hard to patch up old quarrels. Once, after a film session at Denham studios, he gave Frank Probyn a lift to the station. Before Probyn got out of the car Aubrey held him back. "You've been very kind to Dennis. I realize I haven't been kind to you and you could have taken it out on Dennis for what I did." He was referring, of course, to the rivalry over the professorships at the Royal Academy and the Royal College, but he also felt that he owed a debt to Probyn for looking after Dennis in a way that he was no longer able to do himself. Dennis could not be present at his father's funeral and it was particularly appropriate that Leonard should ask Frank Probyn to lead the cortège. Aubrey's last years had been emotionally unhappy, too. His wife Marion had died of a heart attack in February 1954. He had remarried in October of the same year, to Muriel Hart whom he had known in the 1930s in the BBC Symphony Orchestra, but he had little time left in which to enjoy the small consolation she brought into his life.

However sad the story of Aubrey's declining years, his very real contribution to the history of English horn-playing must never be overlooked. Between the two world wars he brought new prestige to the horn as a solo instrument. He demonstrated that 'cracks' and 'bubbles' were the fault of the player, not the instrument, yet he never sacrificed tone quality on the altar of technical brilliance. Those who remember him still thrill at the pure sound he could produce in his heyday, but the penetration of sound he could achieve was in no way limited by the narrow-bore horn, as his many orchestral recordings of works by Richard Strauss and Wagner amply bear out. He was probably one of the greatest orchestral horn-players of all time, and he lived long enough to see his son Dennis assume that mantle and become a virtuoso soloist as well.

ঔ 9 ঌ

Finale

After the death of Aubrey the rest of September and early October was largely taken up with concerts by the Wind Ensemble. There were also recording sessions with the Philharmonia Orchestra to fit in. Between 3 and 7 October Klemperer recorded Beethoven's Third, Seventh and Fifth Symphonies, and then between the 10th and the 12th Karajan recorded Mozart's Symphony no. 39. In the midst of all this hectic activity Dennis was pleased to be able to be home when Yvonne gave birth to their second child, a girl, Sally. He was equally relieved that she had arrived before the Philharmonia's forthcoming tour of the United States. The last of Karajan's Mozart recording sessions had been devoted to the final rehearsals for the tour. It was Karajan's second American visit with a European orchestra in two years: in February and March 1954 he had taken the Berlin Philharmonic on their first American tour. Now it was the turn of the Philharmonia, and Columbia Artists had arranged a four-week tour of the East Coast with a total of twenty-four concerts. On 22 October 106 players left London Airport in two airliners bound for Washington. For Dennis it was his second visit in six years, but this time he was not to play any concertos. The repertoire for the tour was entirely orchestral, though it did contain some works that highlight the horn to a considerable extent, among them Sibelius's Fifth Symphony and Mozart's B♭ Divertimento K 287. The American press certainly did not allow Dennis to go unnoticed. Of the Philharmonia's opening concert in Washington on 23 October the *Post* said:

> The brightness of the slender-bored [*sic*] horns favoured by the discerning Englishmen matches the perfect sheen of the strings. . . . The horn section alone would certainly lift lesser orchestras into first rank.

And in the *Chicago Tribune* on 8 November, Claudia Cassidy wrote of the Philharmonia: "It is a brilliant orchestra with a celestial horn-player named Dennis Brain."

The tour was highly successful but very tiring, and an uncomfortable incident right at the end put a severe strain on the close relations enjoyed by Karajan and the Philharmonia. At the seating rehearsal for the final concert—19 November in Symphony Hall, Boston—a back-desk string player (who had only joined the tour at the last minute to replace someone who was ill) demanded that Karajan should apologize for his habit of disappearing so rapidly at the end of concerts, even before the applause had died away. The Philharmonia was used to this, but to tired players even the smallest irritation becomes disproportionately aggravating. Karajan refused to conduct the evening concert if the player concerned were present, and a number of players, among them Dennis and Gareth Morris, retaliated by saying that they would only play if he were present. After an extremely tense afternoon and a great many telephone calls by the harassed managing director of the orchestra, Jane Withers, the concert did finally take place, with Karajan and with Dennis, Gareth and the others. The strain caused by the incident did not last long, for Karajan took the Philharmonia on a European tour early in 1956 and relations were restored to their former harmony.

Dennis did not go on this tour. In his place was Alan Civil, who had joined the Philharmonia as third horn to go on the USA tour and had very soon after become co-principal with Dennis, under much the same arrangement as in the Royal Philharmonic Orchestra in 1953 and 1954. This allowed Dennis to pursue his solo and Ensemble interests more fully and bring to fruition a number of new ventures. He also wanted to devote more time to his family: he was seldom at home for any length of time as engagements took him all over Britain and Europe. He rarely, if ever, turned down a booking, and many were the days that a morning recording session would be followed by an afternoon rehearsal, an evening concert and then a late-night broadcast recital. The only other bookings with which he filled his diary were for bridge-parties. He and Yvonne were good players and they made up a four as often as they could for a relaxing evening.

Dennis also played chess, which he found both absorbing and relaxing.

A month after the Philharmonia's return from the United States
an interesting concert of new music, sponsored by the Institute of
Contemporary Arts, was held at the Wigmore Hall on 20 December. Three new works were performed, including the first concert
performance of Vaughan Williams' Violin Sonata, by Frederick
Grinke and Michael Mullinar. Equally significant were the first
performances of Michael Tippett's Sonata for four horns and
Gunther Schüller's Five Pieces for five horns. The players were
advertised as the 'Dennis Brain Wind Ensemble', but in fact all
the players came from the Philharmonia horn section, led by
Dennis. The *Musical Times* found the pieces rather tedious, and
it is true that for the general listener the sound of a number of
horns can pall after a while. The Hindemith Sonata for Four
Horns suffered a similar reception. Nevertheless the works were
significant additions to the instrument's repertoire, even though
they are probably of more interest to the performer than the
listener. The same players gave the first broadcast of the Hindemith and Tippett sonatas on 5 January 1956.

In February 1956 Dennis gathered his Trio together again. The
success of their first concert nearly two years before had encouraged him sufficiently to go ahead with the venture on a larger
scale, when time permitted. Now, with Jean Pougnet and Wilfred
Parry as before, he had succeeded in booking, through the services
of the Scottish Arts Council, a tour of Scotland lasting a week.
Dennis contrived things so that the tour linked up with engagements he already had in Scotland. On 22, 24 and 25 February he
played Mozart's Second Concerto and Strauss's First Concerto
with the Scottish National Orchestra in Dundee, Edinburgh and
Glasgow respectively and then met Wilfred Parry for a recital in
St Andrews on the following day. Jean Pougnet joined the two of
them in Aberdeen on the 27th for the start of the tour proper,
with a concert in Markinch on the 28th. The 29th was a particularly busy day. Dennis and Wilfred gave a recital at George
Watson's School, Edinburgh, in the morning, joined Jean for a
lunchtime concert in the Freemasons' Hall, and then all three of
them travelled to Glasgow for another concert in the evening.
The last concert of the tour was on 3 March in a delightful

setting—the Adam-style music-room of Auchinleck House, ancestral home of the Boswell family. The laird, Mr John P. D. Boswell, was host to nearly a hundred members of the Cumnock Music Club. The Trio was an ideal unit for recitals of this kind. It was highly mobile—each member took his own car—and could offer a combination of violin and horn sonatas together with the trios by Brahms and Lennox Berkeley as well as an arrangement, by E. Neumann, of the Mozart Horn Quintet. Wilfred Parry later described the Trio as the most successful ensemble with which he had ever been associated.

Despite the obvious enthusiasm for the new Trio, Dennis's Wind Ensemble still flourished and indeed was particularly busy during these first months of 1956. There were concerts in Dublin and Farnham in January, a Festival Hall concert and another in Brighton in March, in addition to broadcasts in February of wind octets by Uhl and Mozart. One concert which they never forgot was in Saffron Walden, in a local church hall: while the flautist and pianist were performing a flute sonata, the ceiling collapsed and fell onto the piano and the chair on which Dennis had been sitting! With Dennis, Gareth Morris and Cecil James holding full-time orchestral posts in the Philharmonia and Leonard in the Royal Philharmonic, it was always difficult and sometimes impossible to meet for rehearsal before a concert. At a famous girls' public school they were booked for a difficult programme but had no time to go over it before the concert itself. With Dennis in control everything went smoothly until afterwards, at the reception which had been laid on for them. The headmistress, delighted with the whole concert, made straight for Dennis. "How do you all achieve such perfect ensemble?" she asked. Knowing they had not rehearsed, Dennis was somewhat at a loss for words. Seeing his embarrassment, Wilfred Parry came to the rescue. Looking the lady straight in the eye, he replied, "Constant rehearsal, madam." "Of course," said their hostess, "I try to impress that on all our girls." Another concert was at a music club some hundred miles from London, and as Leonard was unavailable, Sidney Sutcliffe (Dennis's colleague in the Philharmonia) offered to help out. After two three-hour recording sessions with the Philharmonia in Kingsway Hall Dennis and Sidney finally got away at about 5.30 pm. While Dennis drove, Sidney changed into his tails in the car, and as soon as they arrived Dennis pushed him onto the platform to sight-read the Ibert Trio!

The Ensemble's first foreign tour was arranged by Dennis through a Mrs Erede in Turin, between 26 March and 11 April 1956. The whole group (the Quintet and Wilfred Parry) travelled overland to Italy in two cars, Dennis's Citroen and Wilfred Parry's Volkswagen. It was a tiring trip; some of them developed sore throats and found relief on the long car journeys only in Stock, the Italian brandy. Their first stop was Milan: the Piccola Scala Theatre had been newly opened that February as a concert-hall and the whole Ensemble gave its first concert there on 26 March. The next day, in the same theatre, Dennis and Gareth played Mozart concertos, separated by a performance of the Sinfonia Concertante K 297b. The remainder of the tour took in Palermo and Messina on 3 and 4 April and Florence, L'Aquila and Rome from the 7th to the 9th and ended in Turin on 11 April. Such was the artistic success of the tour that Mrs Erede arranged a similar tour for Dennis's Trio the following year.

The Ensemble did not return to London until 14 April, and Dennis became immediately involved in the final preparations for his newest project—his own chamber orchestra. It had long been an ambition of his to conduct, and he had at last collected together some of his closest friends into a small orchestra. He asked Jean Pougnet to lead at first, but Pougnet wanted to remain free-lance and was reluctant to return to orchestral playing. Instead, Dennis chose his colleague from the Philharmonia, Hugh Bean; indeed, many of the players came from the ranks of the Philharmonia. There were two desks each of first violins, second violins, violas and 'cellos, and one desk of double-basses. Dennis's step-mother was in the viola section and Leonard as oboist completed the family involvement. The first concert was on 18 April in the Wigmore Hall, and at this, as at subsequent concerts, Dennis both played and conducted. The programme for the orchestra's début contained one modern work, Fricker's Concertante for cor anglais and strings, which Leonard played; the rest was entirely devoted to Mozart. Dennis conducted the early Symphony no. 17 in G and the F major Divertimento K 247, and played the First Horn Concerto and the Fragment in E. *The Times* spoke highly of the concert as a whole, praising Dennis's playing as "bravura that wears a swagger grin, a quality conveyed to perfection in Mr Brain's virtuosity and sense of humour" and of his conducting wrote that: "A more experienced conductor would have controlled the flow of Fricker's piece so that its shape was more clearly shown; otherwise Mr Brain was content to beat time for his skilful players. The *Daily Telegraph* made perhaps the best evaluation:

. . . conducted by Dennis Brain who perhaps has, like other great artists before him, begun to fret under the limited repertory of works he can play himself.

No technical virtuoso with the baton, he directed his players in a programme largely devoted to Mozart with clear, unadorned gestures and was rewarded with some playing of much the same nature. He was also the soloist, as impeccable as always, in Mozart's D major concerto K 412.

It was undoubtedly true that Dennis was always looking for new ways of widening his musical interests, and many of his friends had noticed a growing restlessness—a key factor in the formation of his orchestra. He once or twice complained that he could never make a fortune playing the horn, compared with say a top pianist or violinist, but in reality he was completely indifferent to money. It bought food and cars! His prime aim was always to enjoy making music with his close friends and colleagues, and while he was perhaps not ruthless enough to become a great conductor he achieved excellent results with precise, unaffected gestures that were appreciated by those who played for him. Two more concerts closely followed the Wigmore Hall début: on 22 April the venue was the Conway Hall, the programme the same as that on the 18th except that the Third Mozart Horn Concerto replaced the First and the C minor Serenade the Divertimento. Then there was a second Wigmore Hall concert on 27 April which included three Mozart items, the Second Horn Concerto, the K 334 Divertimento in D major and Symphony no. 11 in D, plus Malcolm Arnold's Sinfonietta in F. One paper commented about the last item that "Dennis Brain hardly seemed necessary": he certainly found conducting harder work than he had imagined it to be, but from now on he devoted a large part of his time and energy to his orchestra and derived a great deal of pleasure from it.

On 29 April Dennis gave the first performance of a new horn concerto by Anthony Lewis, at the Victoria and Albert Museum.

The Boyd Neel Orchestra was conducted by Brian Priestman and, though the concerto was not particularly tuneful, its striking design was well received. Anthony Lewis had earlier written a trumpet concerto for the Proms and had wanted to write a work for the horn. Dennis was the obvious choice for its first performance and gladly accepted the dedication. He asked for no alterations to Lewis's score except to the long note at the end of the slow movement, for which he needed time to take a breath. The concerto in fact received two 'first' performances: Stravinsky's Concerto in D for strings was withdrawn from the programme at the last moment and this gave an ideal opportunity for Dennis to play the new horn concerto again in the second half.

The last day of April 1956 saw Dennis back at the Wigmore Hall for the Tenth Anniversary Concert of his Wind Ensemble. The concert had a second purpose, to raise funds for a projected Aubrey Brain Memorial Scholarship for wind-players. With this in mind, Dennis asked Gordon Jacob to write a piece for the occasion, which he did, a Sextet for piano and wind. In the score that was published later, Jacob wrote of the work:

> This was written in memory of Aubrey Brain, the great horn-player and father of the equally distinguished Dennis Brain. The musical notes A B E B A taken from the name Aubrey Brain are used as a thematic basis for all the movements except the *cortège* which however is in B♭ minor and is therefore centred round the note B♭, thus bringing into prominence the initial B.

The result was a highly imaginative piece that combined elegiac grace with wit and vivacity and has retained an important place in the repertoire. At the concert Dennis also played York Bowen's Sonata which Bowen, who played the piano part, had written for Aubrey in 1938. The remaining works, a modern quartet by Ghedini, a Partita for wind by Denis Matthews and Dennis's own arrangement for wind quartet of Mozart's F minor Fantasia, were all in birthday vein and of birthday standard. It was appropriate that Wilfred Parry and George Malcolm, the pianists with whom the Ensemble had been associated, should have taken part on this occasion, assisting as accompanists.

At the end of May, at recording sessions for the Philharmonia, Cantelli conducted Beethoven's Fifth and Seventh Symphonies.

These were the climax of nearly five years' association between the Philharmonia and the young Italian: five years that had witnessed some stormy and emotional scenes but had also produced some fabulous recordings, such as Wagner's Siegfried Idyll and Brahams's First and Third Symphonies, to say nothing of some excellent Debussy performances. Tragically, these were Cantelli's last sessions with the Philharmonia, and the recording of the Fifth Symphony, which had promised to be one of the finest ever, was never completed: Cantelli was killed in an air crash over Paris the following November. Only two movements had been recorded and the slow movement was issued soon after on a commemorative disc.

During the recording sessions Dennis gave another new work its London première. This was the Arioso and Scherzo by Arnold Cooke, which he played with the Carter String Trio and Marjorie Lempfert (viola) at the Wigmore Hall on 26 May. The work has the same scoring as the Mozart K 407 Horn Quintet, for horn, violin, two violas and 'cello, and had been written for Dennis and the Carter Trio at the suggestion of Mrs Hackforth, the wife of a Cambridge don. She ran a concert society known as the Thursday Concerts Society and it was at one of their concerts that Dennis had given the first performance early in 1955, soon after Cooke had completed it. After the London première Dennis recorded the work a number of times for the BBC. Later, he asked Cooke to rescore it for violin, horn and piano, obviously with Trio concerts in mind, but this was never accomplished.

On 31 May Dennis called in at Covent Garden on his way to another engagement to play Siegfried's horn-call from Act II of Wagner's *Siegfried*. He had played the horn-call twice before at Covent Garden, in 1954 and 1955. On this occasion Rudolf Kempe was the conductor, with Wolfgang Windgassen making his début in the title role, and before Dennis could slip away he had been noticed by Noel Goodwin of the *Daily Express*, who wrote:

Hidden offstage was another star of the evening—our own expert horn-player Dennis Brain, whose immaculate playing of Siegfried's horn-call (his signature tune) was a marvel.

The words in brackets call for some explanation. The horn-call had become Dennis's signature tune through his contribution to

K

HMV's *Instruments of the Orchestra* records made with Sir Malcolm Sargent in May 1947; since then he had played it at many concerts. Beecham, in particular, came to give Dennis the nickname 'Siegfried of the horn'. It was no novelty for Dennis to play more than one engagement in an evening. He once played the Quoniam from Bach's B minor Mass and a concerto at different concerts on one night, with the aid of a taxi in between. The story is also told of a provincial concert at which Dennis was playing two concertos, which were separated by a symphony and the interval. During the interval he was missing from the artists' room and somebody jokingly suggested, "He's probably giving a half-hour recital at the BBC." Dennis was! Far from being an exceptional story, this is only too true of Dennis's pace of work generally: he seemed tireless, yet always relaxed, and never liked to let anyone down by refusing an engagement.

The tenor Peter Pears had for a number of years appeared at the Holland Festival, and in 1956 he was joined by Dennis and Benjamin Britten for a joint recital—yet another festival for Dennis to add to the list of those at which he had played. The programme, given in the small hall of the Concertgebouw in Amsterdam on 6 June, was as remarkable for its variety as for the sheer stamina it demanded of Dennis, who had to play his way through Schubert's "Auf dem Strom", Britten's "Still Falls the Rain", Dukas's *Villanelle* and Schumann's Adagio and Allegro. The only concession Dennis allowed himself was about half-a-dozen bars' rest in the Allegro of the Schumann, where the melody was given to the piano. As with the Serenade Dennis's performances of "Still Falls the Rain" gave this new work the impetus it needed to become firmly established in the repertoire. Only a fortnight after the Holland performance he played it again with Pears and Britten at the Aldeburgh Festival: on 22 June the BBC relayed a programme entitled "The Heart of the Matter", a miscellany of poems by Edith Sitwell, read by the author herself, and Britten's settings of three of them for tenor, horn and piano. In addition to "Still Falls the Rain", "Fire" and "So, Out Of the Dark" were performed and the programme was framed by a fanfare for solo horn, much in the style of the Serenade. Another new work, the Horn Sonata by Fricker, was given a welcome stimulus by Dennis and Wilfred Parry, who performed it for the first time on the air on 27 June.

A further chance to play it came at the ISCM Festival in Venice in September, to which Dennis's Ensemble had been invited. As well as Fricker's Sonata they gave his Wind Quintet, together with the first performance of Dialogue no. 4 for wind by Malipiero and Riegger's Concerto for piano and wind. The pianist for this recital was Rosalyn Tureck.

On his return from the Venice Festival Dennis recorded the two Strauss Horn Concertos for Columbia at their Abbey Road studios on two consecutive days—21 and 22 September. Wolfgang Sawallisch conducted the Philharmonia Orchestra. The following month Klemperer began to record the complete Brahms symphonies with the same orchestra. In the middle of these sessions Klemperer had to go suddenly to Munich, where his wife had died; for the remaining sessions in November, Hindemith came to London to record a series of his own works with the Philharmonia, and Dennis at last put onto disc the Hindemith Horn Concerto with the composer himself, in a much happier collaboration than with Klemperer in 1954.

Dennis had changed the name of his Trio from the Dennis Brain Trio to a more old-fashioned, but more modest, form—the Brain-Pougnet-Parry Trio. They made a second tour in October 1956, this time of Yorkshire and Lincolnshire. Of the recital they gave on 18 October in York the *Yorkshire Evening Post* wrote:

> One had opportunity to admire the quiet virtuosity of Mr Brain playing and phrasing quick passages on the horn as if it was just a matter of flicking a hand across a keyboard. This concert was certainly one of the best of its kind in recent years and showed the enthusiasm for and enjoyment to be had from listening to first-rate ensembles.

For the first time the BBC took an active interest in the Trio, recording their concert on 25 October in Barton-on-Humber and broadcast it on 28 November. The programme, as nearly always, ended with the Brahms Trio, and Dennis played it from memory, as he did all the standard repertory works. In order to maintain uniformity with the violinist and pianist, both of whom used their copies of the music, Dennis would bring on a completely different piece and put it on his stand. For any horn-players who might be in the audience he even went to the lengths of turning over the pages at the appropriate times!

For many of the Trio and Ensemble concerts Dennis supplied handwritten programme notes for the benefit of the society organizing the event. This led to occasional embarrassment as his handwriting was not very legible. At one concert, in Newbury, Wilfred Parry had to announce to the audience that one item on the programme, which was described as An Oubradous, was in fact the result of Dennis's bad writing and should read Arr. (i.e. arranged by) Oubradous. This was the source of a great deal of amusement, not least to the composer, Gerald Finzi; he was in the audience and came round to see Dennis in the interval and asked him "What is an Oubradous?"

The famous Hoffnung Festival concert on 13 November 1956 gave Dennis a double opportunity to indulge both his expertise and sense of fun. Malcolm Arnold had written a "Grand Grand Overture" especially for the occasion: it included an organ part, and Dennis was able to play his favourite instrument for once. Later in the concert he played a Concerto for Alphorn and Strings, by Leopold Mozart, on a length of garden hosepipe. Behind the obvious humour of the performance was a practical demonstration of Dennis's insistence that the sound a horn-player produced was first and foremost the product of the physical make-up of the player himself. Even on a hosepipe, as he often showed in lecture-recitals, he was able to convey his own style and tone quality in a way that was quickly appreciated by the listener.

Dennis was now becoming a familiar personality on both radio and television. His radio broadcasts, in particular, were not confined to studio performances as soloist or ensemble player. Mention has already been made of his Third Programme talk on the early horn in July 1955, and earlier than that, in August 1953, he had appeared on a quiz programme, "What Do You Know?". In July 1956 he introduced "On a Personal Note"—a programme of horn music which he compiled, reading his own script. Then on 13 August he was Roy Plomley's guest in the popular and long-running programme "Desert Island Discs". Listeners were given a fascinating insight into his personality and views on music generally. What guided his choice of eight records was that they were works he was not likely to have played or be called upon to play.

His own record collection was largely of artists for whom he had a great admiration, players such as Heifetz, Moiseiwitch, in particular. He also only chose one orchestral record, saying that he could carry most of the well-known symphonies and concertos in his head. Instead he selected records by Heifetz, from whom he always said he had learnt a great deal, and works that had personal significance—Frank Sinatra singing "You Go to my Head", which was one of Yvonne's favourites; two jazz records, "Horn-belt Boogie" by Mitch Miller and "We'll Get It" played by Tommy Dorsey, which reflected his love of lighter music and, in the latter case, recalled New York and his winter of 1944–5 in the USA with the RAF, and "Down by the Sally Gardens", as arranged by Britten, in which he paid tribute to the composer of the Serenade.

One fascinating broadcast, given on 17 December on the Third Programme, featured Dennis in a unique performance. Earlier in 1956 the conductor Charles Mackerras had gone to Germany to visit the Furstenberg Library at Donauerschingen. There he found and filmed a number of rare works, hitherto unpublished and never performed in England. One such, which had lain silent in manuscript form since the composer's own day, was Haydn's Concert Trio Pietà di Me in E♭ major. Scored for two sopranos and tenor with orchestra it has obbligato parts for cor anglais, bassoon and horn; the solo horn part is staggeringly difficult, possibly the most difficult ever written, rising frequently to the E♭ and F above the top C normally prescribed as the upper limit for the instrument. In the studio were assembled Joan Sutherland and April Cantelo (sopranos), Raymond Nilsson (tenor), with Peter Graeme (cor anglais), John Alexandra (bassoon) and the Goldsbrough Orchestra conducted by Charles Mackerras. The work had been transposed down to D major to make the horn part more easily playable, but even so Dennis inwardly quailed at the thought of a live performance. Nevertheless he approached it half-humorously treating the whole thing as a joke while in reality minding desperately that it was not going as well as it should: some of the highest notes were occasionally fluffed, but the whole part was suffused with such panache and sense of style that he carried it through.

In December there were three more significant concerts. Perhaps the most interesting was that on 4 December in Paris,

Dennis's only appearance there as a soloist. He had played there with the Philharmonia Orchestra twice in 1952, and his only solo performances anywhere in France had been at Aix-en-Provence in 1948 and 1954. The French did not think much of his style of playing the horn (nor, frankly, did Dennis think much of theirs) so it is not surprising that, having invited Manoug Parikian and Lamar Crowson, the Société Philharmonique was reluctant to take up Parikian's suggestion to invite Dennis as well, to perform the Brahms Trio. Parikian insisted and the Société agreed, rather unwillingly. A radio recording was also arranged; this turned out to be the worst-balanced Brahms Trio the three of them had ever heard, entirely through the incompetence of the balance engineer. Despite these drawbacks it was a most enjoyable trip and Dennis was particularly pleased because Yvonne had been able to come with them. Ten days later, he appeared just one more time for the Royal Philharmonic Orchestra and Beecham. It was nearly three years since he had finally left the orchestra, although he had rejoined them for a very few recording sessions. On 12 December, in the Royal Festival Hall, he headed no less than eight horns in a performance of Beethoven's "Choral" Symphony. Then on 28 December he was able to pay tribute to another of his musical heroes, Pablo Casals, on the eve of the 'cellist's eightieth birthday. The whole concert, at the Friends' Meeting House, Euston Road, was organized to raise money for the Pablo Casals Eightieth Birthday Fund: Dennis's contribution was a Mozart horn concerto, no. 3 in E♭, and others taking part were the London Bach Group and the Collegium Musicum Londinii conducted by John Munchinton.

Dennis now had a new car, a green TR2 sports no. SXX 3 which he had bought the previous June. It made light work of the frequent long journeys between engagements. He soon had his leg pulled about it: at a party he was talking with someone he had met in the USA on the RAF tour and had to admit that, although he had spent seven years in the RAF, he had never flown himself. "Don't let him kid you," someone interrupted. "He flies in that new sports car of his!" Dennis was not best pleased, however, that for his Trio's second tour of Scotland in March 1957 they were not able to use their own cars: petrol rationing following the Suez crisis had made motoring a luxury, and as each liked to use his own car the only practical solution seemed to be a hired car and chauffeur for the whole trip. This time the tour took them from Fort William to Helensburgh by way of towns as far apart as Elgin and Campbeltown. As on many trips, Dennis took his camera: he was very keen on photography and skilful, too, with a good eye for a picture. He had begun to experiment with colour photography, with some fine results, and one of his earliest successes was an amusing shot of Wilfred Parry propping up the bar in a Scottish hotel, wearing a kilt! The tour was an even greater success than the first, filling local halls to capacity to hear what Dennis described to the press as 'highly intellectual pieces'. All except one of the twelve concerts ended with the Brahms Trio; Jean Pougnet's contributions were the Schubert Sonatina in D, Debussy's G minor Sonata and the Beethoven op. 12 no. 1 Sonata in D, while Dennis offered Dukas's *Villanelle*, Beethoven's op. 17 Sonata and Neumann's trio arrangement of the Mozart K 407 Horn Quintet. The exception, the last concert, on 25 March in the Victoria Halls, Helensburgh, was a joint concert with the local music society. Wilfred Parry played some solos by Schumann, Chopin and Rachmaninov and accompanied the tenor, Daniel McCoshan, in some songs; he and Dennis then joined for Strauss's First Concerto, *Villanelle* and Beethoven's Horn Sonata. This concert was almost the end of the Trio for they only appeared together once more, on 28 March at Welwyn Garden City. Jean Pougnet was suffering increasingly from cramp in his left arm, and all three felt it best that they should suspend their activities for a while. They never met as the Brain-Pougnet-Parry Trio again.

Work in the Philharmonia was as demanding as ever: in addition to the regular London concerts there was a heavy recording programme. In mid-February Constantin Silvestri recorded the last three Tchaikovsky symphonies, and at the end of March Klemperer completed his cycle of Brahms's symphonies. Dennis found it increasingly difficult to maintain his commitments to the Philharmonia and carry out a full programme of solo engagements without sacrificing even more of the little time he was able to spend at home with his family. He never mentioned the possibility of retiring from full-time orchestral playing, but more and more frequently he made use of Aubrey Thonger as a 'bumper-up'. He had not gone on the Philharmonia's tour of Europe at the be-

ginning of 1956 and he similarly forewent a tour of Ireland in
May 1957. Alan Civil was co-principal with Dennis and recalls their
months together in the Philharmonia with great affection and,
on occasion, some amusement. He had been asked by the BBC
to play the Beethoven Sextet op. 81b for a broadcast recital in
February 1957: both horn parts are extremely tricky and at
Philharmonia rehearsals he spent a good deal of time going over
the more hazardous passages. A week or so before the day of the
broadcast he telephoned the BBC to confirm the recital and asked,
"By the way, who is playing second horn?" "Oh, you are," came
the reply. "Dennis Brain is the other player." Alan Civil's embarrassment can be imagined, for he had spent days practising the
first horn part well within earshot of Dennis!

While the Philharmonia were in Ireland, Dennis was in the
middle of a busy schedule of solo engagements. On 26 May he
played Haydn's First Concerto and the Gordon Bryan Concerto
at St John's College, Cambridge, with the Harvey Phillips Orchestra. Their leader was Hugh Bean, who, as well as leading Dennis's
new chamber orchestra, had since February been deputy leader
of the Philharmonia. Dennis took his chamber orchestra to the
1957 Aldeburgh Festival where he conducted them in works by
Telemann, Mozart, Stravinsky and Fricker, as well as playing
Haydn's First Concerto and the Mozart Fragment in E. That night
he drove straight home as usual after the concert; not a long
distance, but far enough after a heavy day's rehearsing, playing
and conducting. The following evening he made two appearances
with the BBC Concert Orchestra and Vilem Tausky in "At Home",
a miscellany of lighter classical pieces. As well as the slow movement from Mozart's Third Concerto he played Gilbert Vinter's
Hunter's Moon, an attractive little work written for John Burden during the war and which Dennis had played and broadcast a number of times over the years, including a television performance in the Vera Lynn show on 7 May 1957.

For the Light Music Festival of 1957 the BBC had commissioned
Ernest Tomlinson to write a work for horn, the timing of which
had been specified. Tomlinson planned a Romance and Rondo and
suggested Dennis as the first performer; the producer's immediate
reaction was, "Well, don't write it so that only Dennis Brain can
play it." This advice Tomlinson promptly ignored on the principle

that if you are going to write for a virtuoso, you do just that. He also quoted, towards the end of the Rondo, part of the theme from the last movement of Mozart's Fourth Horn Concerto with which Dennis was now firmly associated through popular record programmes. It was Tomlinson's first contact with Dennis, and, when he rang him to tell him he wanted to write a Rondo, Dennis said, "Oh, I hope it's not a 6/8 rondo: there are far too many of them." The Rondo was in fact in 2/4 time, and when the main themes had been sketched out Tomlinson sent them to Dennis to see if they were suitable. They met in the interval of a recording session at Walthamstow Town Hall and Tomlinson was delighted that Dennis had only the slightest of modifications to suggest, and none at all for the main theme. At the first run-through with orchestra Tomlinson was pleased with the way things were going. At the first stop, however, Dennis immediately turned to him and said, "Ernest, you'll have to do it a lot faster than that. I've been practising it at this speed," and proceeded to play it. This suited Tomlinson perfectly as it was an occupational hazard trying to get his pieces played fast enough! The orchestra blenched a little but were pacified somewhat when it was pointed out to them that nothing they had been given was more difficult than the music Dennis had to play, and he was doing it on a horn. On the night itself, 22 June in the Royal Festival Hall, the piece, conducted by Tomlinson himself, was received rapturously.

Yet another 'first' came on 17 July at the Cheltenham Festival, when Malcolm Arnold conducted Dennis and the Hallé Orchestra in the première of his Second Horn Concerto. Arnold and Dennis had been old friends and colleagues since the London Baroque Ensemble concerts in 1949 at which they had both played; they had also broadcast together several times. Arnold's First Horn Concerto had been performed in London in 1946 by Charles Gregory, for whom it had been written; Gregory was Arnold's colleague in the London Philharmonic Orchestra in the days when Arnold was still an orchestral trumpet-player. Dennis gave the first broadcast performance of the concerto with Gilbert Vinter in May 1951. It is sad to think that the first, and as it happened the only, performance of Arnold's second concerto was the only concert the BBC did not record at the Cheltenham Festival. According to the *Daily Telegraph*, the work "was splendidly played by

Dennis Brain who received a great ovation with the composer who conducted his own music". The concerto had been written during the last months of 1956 and exploited Dennis's talents to the full. In particular the slow movement was designed solely to highlight his superb cantabile playing, which is one of the most difficult aspects of all wind-playing.

Summer 1957 promised to be an outstanding one for Dennis's Ensemble. They were booked to play at both the Salzburg and Edinburgh Festivals, their first appearance at each—an important milestone in the Ensemble's international reputation. The Salzburg concert was on 30 July, and Dennis made the long journey there and back by car. In the Mozarteum they played Mozart's Piano and Wind Quintet and the Wind Quintet K 270, as well as Poulenc's Sextet and Hindemith's *Kleine Kammermusik* op. 24 no. 2. Karajan, whose first year this was as artistic director of the Festival, was present in the audience together with many other famous performers and conductors. To Dennis their presence caused no alarm, nor did it arouse the slightest arrogance; he never failed to show genuine amazement that such people should take the trouble to come and hear him play. Then there was Edinburgh. The first of the two concerts, on 22 August, had the same programme as at Salzburg. Acoustically, the Usher Hall was not ideally suited to such a small group, but the quality of the performance provided ample compensation. The *Scotsman* described the concert as "a mixture of Mozart and the not-too-moderns" and "one of those oases of rest and refreshment which the kindly authorities place along the Festival highway". On 24 August the venue was the Freemasons' Hall, eminently more suitable particularly since the piano was again involved, this time in Beethoven's op. 16 Quintet. Wind quintets by Malipiero and Fricker framed the only solo Dennis allowed himself, the Dukas *Villanelle*, which he played "with debonair ease, and proved it to be a charming *bonne bouche*". So charmed were the audience that they demanded an encore, and as they went back on stage Wilfred Parry whispered to Dennis "You had better announce it"; it was their regular encore, a piece called "Le Basque" by Marin Marais and originally composed for the viola. Dennis whispered back "No repeats," and they went on. He rarely announced items, but he broke his accustomed modesty and told the audience that he would play them "a little French dance, which also happens to be the shortest piece I know".

While they were in Edinburgh Dennis spent many hours at the offices of the Scottish Arts Council arranging a tour of Scotland for his chamber orchestra in late September. It was a project very close to his heart and he and Mrs Spink and her staff worked hard to make the necessary arrangements. Seven concerts were planned for the week of 25 September to 3 October and he was to discuss the final arrangements when he came back to Edinburgh the following week to play with the Philharmonia Orchestra. After the concert on the morning of the 26 August he drove Leonard back to London. Just before they left, Wilfred Parry asked Dennis if he would book him a room at a Doncaster hotel. Dennis pulled a wry face, complaining that the stop would ruin his average speed for the journey, but he only spoke in fun. Leonard remembered that drive well. Dennis never took any unnecessary risks, holding back on many an occasion when Leonard confessed that he himself would have overtaken. Leonard had to be back for two Prom concerts with the Royal Philharmonic Orchestra, while Dennis had three days of rehearsal with the Philharmonia in preparation for the Edinburgh concerts. In the midst of these he was busy with future plans for the Ensemble: on the Tuesday he rang Wilfred Parry to tell him of the progress he had made in arranging a tour of Australia for them and promised to tell him more about it when they met next. He was also preoccupied with his chamber orchestra and had just completed an arrangement of the National Anthem for them.

Dennis then drove north again to Edinburgh. The Philharmonia had three concerts in the Festival on the last three days of August, all in the Usher Hall. At the rehearsal for the first of these, Mozart's Symphony no. 29 and Mahler's *Das Lied von der Erde* with Klemperer, Dennis fell asleep momentarily: the hectic work of the past weeks and months was beginning to have its effect. Rafael Kubelik conducted Friday's concert, with Dvořák's Symphonic Variations and Beethoven's Fifth Symphony framing a new work by Martinu for piano (with Rudolf Firkusny). The concert on Saturday the 31st was an all-Tchaikovsky programme, conducted by Eugene Ormandy. The Philharmonia rehearsed a full three hours in the Usher Hall that morning. In the break Dennis sought out Ormandy to discuss with him the following Friday's concert when

he was to play the Strauss Second Concerto with the Concertgebouw Orchestra. Ormandy noticed how tired Dennis looked and
begged him to take things more easily, but he just smiled and
shrugged his shoulders. Walter Legge also noticed that Dennis was
tired and advised him to rest that afternoon, but Dennis was away
playing at a lecture-recital. He did manage to have a quick nap in
the hotel before the concert as he planned to drive home through
the night after the concert. It would be quicker than the train,
which he found tiring anyway, and he could be home for an early
breakfast with Yvonne and the children.

During the interval of the Ormandy concert he admitted to
one of his colleagues that he was not looking forward to the drive
home, a most unusual remark. After the concert he made his way
out of the Usher Hall, stopping briefly to remind a friend that
they were meeting for lunch in Edinburgh the following Friday. He
climbed into his TR2 and dropped his instrument onto the back
seat of the car. He spotted Hugh Bean, heading for a nightcap before closing-time. "Do you want to see the new National Anthem
arrangement?" he called. "I've got it in the car." "Not now,"
Hugh called back. "See you about it on Monday." Several of his
Philharmonia colleagues stopped to chat to him before making for
the pubs, their hotel or, as in the case of the other four horn-
players, for the overnight train. With a wave and a chuckle Dennis
set off on the 380-mile journey home.

✐ 10 ✐

Aftermath—
Still Falls the Rain

At about 6.00 am on Sunday morning, 1 September 1957, a couple were driving north in a van along the A1 Barnet by-pass. It was raining heavily and visibility was very bad. On the dual carriageway, near the main De Havillands factory, they saw the lights of a car approaching very fast in the opposite direction. Just by Wellfield Road, on a bend, it suddenly left the road and mounted the grass verge. Its lights flickered out for a moment, came on again and then finally went out as the car overturned and smashed into an elm. Trapped inside the car, Dennis Brain was dead.

When P.C. Harris arrived on the scene some eight minutes later he was unable, even after righting the car, to remove Dennis. The fire-brigade had to be called and only after part of the car had been cut away with oxy-acetylene equipment could he be removed. Glass and bits of the car were scattered over a distance of nearly fifty yards. The car itself was a complete wreck and one of the springs had disintegrated, three leaves embedding themselves into the tree to quite a depth. Dennis's horn lay smashed on the grass, a little way from the car.

The listeners to the eight o'clock news that Sunday morning received the news that Dennis was dead with horrified disbelief. It tore at the heart of every music-lover in the land. For those most closely involved personally, the very suddenness of the fatal accident had a numbing effect; on none more so than Yvonne, waiting just seventeen miles away for Dennis to reach home in time for breakfast. She was so affected that it was left to Leonard to break the news to Dennis's closest friends and colleagues. When Frank Probyn's telephone rang that Sunday morning he knew when he heard Leonard's voice what he was going to say. "It's Dennis, isn't it?" he asked. "Something's happened." The news that it had, that the young man who sat beside him for so many concerts and record sessions, who always called him *Mr* Probyn and looked upon him with special affection, that he would play no more made him ill for the rest of the day. Wilfred Parry, who was recording for the BBC in their Glasgow studios, learnt the news quite by chance. The conductor, Ian Whyte, knew and was determined to keep it from Wilfred until after the recording, but a player in the orchestra was chatting to him just before they were due to start and happened to mention, "Isn't it awful about Dennis?" It was with the greatest difficulty that Wilfred continued with the recording. The numbing shock was felt by all, from his closest family and colleagues to the countless listeners to the radio news bulletin.

The deep sense of personal loss was quickly followed by realization of the musical implications of Dennis's death. At the time the reaction was perhaps nowhere keener felt than in Edinburgh. Eugene Ormandy recalled sadly the warning he had given Dennis only the day before, to take life more easily. "Britain and the world have lost a great person," he reflected, and Robert Ponsonby, Artistic Administrator of the Edinburgh Festival, added, "Mr Brain will be mourned throughout the world of music, not least in Edinburgh where he had many friends and to whose Festival he contributed so much." Indeed, on Monday morning, the first active musical tribute came from Edinburgh: in the Freemasons' Hall the Deller Consort sang Tallis's "Salvator Mundi", their opening motet, in memory of Dennis. In London, Walter Legge faced a stunned Philharmonia Orchestra in Kingsway Hall, assembled for the first recording sessions of Strauss's *Capriccio* with Sawallisch. The photographer Eric Auerbach was there to take pictures of the rehearsals and recalls vividly the short speech that Legge made, followed by the uncomfortable moments as Alan Civil moved into the first horn chair and the rest of the horn section was reshuffled to suit him. That evening the Royal Philharmonic Orchestra was appearing at the Proms with Basil Cameron. One of the items on the programme was Tchaikovsky's Sixth Symphony, the last work Dennis had played in Edinburgh on Saturday night. As a mark of respect, and as a token of the esteem in which Dennis was held by the musical world, the audience was requested not to applaud. The work was received in absolute silence. His loss was keenly felt on the Continent too: in Vienna one company put Dennis's Mozart concerto record on display in their windows, mounted on black crêpe. This was a significant tribute for it demonstrated that, though some parts of Europe, notably France and Vienna, did not wholly approve of Dennis's style of playing, they had unreserved respect for him as an artist and deep affection for him as a person.

On Tuesday Eugene Ormandy held a press conference in Edinburgh. Dennis had been due to return to the Festival on Friday 6 September to pay the Strauss Second Horn Concerto with the Concertgebouw and this gap had now to be filled. Ormandy had difficulty controlling the emotion in his voice as he made the announcement and several times had to clear his throat.

We had several plans when making arrangements for altering the programme in which Dennis Brain was to have been soloist. The news of his death was so shocking we did not know what the right thing would be to do. The suggestion was made that since his life was unfinished we should play the "Unfinished" Symphony by Schubert. We are paying our respects to a very great artist and a very great Englishman whose loss will be felt not only in this country but throughout the whole world. As a soloist Dennis Brain had no peer.

The public was asked not to applaud, and a note to this effect was put in the programme for the concert. On Friday night 2500 people stood in silent tribute in the Usher Hall: many of the men wore dark suits and some had red roses in their buttonholes. Eugene Ormandy stood with head bowed. It was one of the most poignant moments of all the eleven Edinburgh Festivals so far held.

While the world of music paid tribute, more mundane events took their course. On the Wednesday the inquest on Dennis's accident was held at Hertford. Yvonne was still too shocked to attend. The coroner was told of Dennis's skill as a driver—"the finest I have ridden with," testified Leonard. The wife of the van driver who witnessed the accident was called and the only possible verdict, accidental death, was recorded. The actual cause remains a mystery to this day. Leonard's first reaction had been that Dennis had dozed at the wheel, a view supported by Dennis's unusual tiredness that week, but much later he suggested that on the very wet road the car might have 'aquaplaned', that is, lost road adhesion and become uncontrollable. Considerable significance was placed at the time on a long scratch mark found leading from the point where the car left the road to the scene of the wreck, and it was suggested that the propeller shaft had fractured. Whatever the cause, Dennis was dead and no amount of speculation would replace him.

The funeral, at Hampstead Parish Church on the afternoon of Friday the 6th, was attended by a large congregation which included many leading figures from the world of music. Walter Legge (for EMI), Myers Foggin and Norman Millar (for the Royal Philharmonic Orchestra), Dr Thomas Armstrong (Royal Academy of Music) and Mr Edward Walker (Royal College of Music) were present as well as many members of the leading London orchestras, in particular the Philharmonia and the BBC Symphony. The BBC itself paid tribute by sending a wreath. The service was led by Canon Alan Rogers, assisted by the Reverend A. C. Heath who gave the address.

From the many press tributes it is perhaps worth gathering together a few extracts which summarize the reaction to Dennis's death. Nearly all mentioned his love of fast cars, but only two actually attributed to this some blame for his accident. Thomas Heinitz, in the American *Saturday Review*, spoke of "Another young musician of priceless talent . . . wantonly sacrificed on the altar of modern high-speed transport", and *The Times* commented that "his insensitivity to risk seems to have exacted a heavy price". *The Times* also mentioned Aubrey and observed that Dennis "was a better player than his father, on the father's own testimony, which is saying a lot", while the *Daily Express* wrote "some were ready to rate him best in the world" and doubted whether he had ever had a single adverse press criticism. Comments on his technique we shall deal with in the final chapter. If one had to single out from all the thousands of words written in tribute, some over-emotional, some misguided or ill-informed, just two facets of Dennis's career which all agreed made him irreplaceable, they would be these. His unique artistry was a constant inspiration to contemporary composers to write new works for the horn's limited repertoire, and to the end he maintained a completely unspoilt charm and modesty in spite of the immense fame and various distinctions that came his way.

When a solo artist dies suddenly it is relatively easy to alter the various engagements that were planned in advance, provided they are limited to purely solo appearances. Concerts such as that conducted by Ormandy at the Edinburgh Festival on 6 September and a Royal Festival Hall performance of Mozart's Fourth Horn Concerto with the Jacques Orchestra planned for 24 September could be re-arranged at short notice, tragic though the circumstances were. Dennis, however, had many varied interests and had spent much of his last weeks planning tours and concerts for his Ensemble and Chamber Orchestra. The projected tour of Scotland by the Chamber Orchestra at the end of September, on which he had worked so hard, had to be cancelled, and the orchestra itself was disbanded after only ever having given four concerts. It was the unanimous wish of both Yvonne and its members that the Ensemble should continue, with its original name: Neill Sanders took over as horn-player, and he left the Philharmonia soon afterwards to work as a freelance. By a happy chance, the Ensemble could be heard on the radio once more with Dennis, on Thursday 5 September. The BBC had originally planned a live recital of the Gordon Jacob Sextet, Mozart's Divertimento in B♭ K 270 and Ibert's *Three Short Pieces*, but Dennis had written to them earlier in the year to ask if they might pre-record the recital as he knew he would be busy with the Philharmonia Orchestra at recording sessions for *Capriccio*. The recital was recorded on 22 July. The Ensemble continued its activities, directed now by Leonard, until the mid-1960s, when a combination of ill-health, other musical commitments and some personal frictions brought about its demise. Like Dennis, whose personality it enshrined, it had reached its zenith while still in the full flower of youth: its influence on music for its own medium was incalculable and its high standards paved the way both for the many excellent groups we enjoy today and for the wider audience for such music.

Dennis had planned a six-week tour of Canada with Denis Matthews to start soon after the end of the Edinburgh Festival and the proposed tour of Scotland with his Chamber Orchestra. The tour had been the brainchild of Jack Barwick, a Canadian with deep-rooted British affiliations. Married to a harpsichordist, he

L

had become disillusioned with the United States' control of musical life in Canada. There was little chance for English artists to go to Canada except via the USA. Barwick therefore set up an agency in Ottawa to import artists direct from England. He received some support from music societies in Canada and from the Canadian Broadcasting Commission. In July 1957 he had met Dennis Brain and Denis Matthews in London and booked them for a tour of Canada: Dennis would play horn concertos with local orchestras, Denis Matthews would give piano recitals, and they would combine at regular intervals for a repertoire that included Dukas's *Villanelle*, Schumann's Adagio and Allegro and the sonatas by Fricker, Hindemith and Beethoven. After Dennis died Barwick still wanted to go ahead with a tour. Another wind-player had to be found, and Leon Goossens the oboist happened to be available. In late October 1957 Goossens and Matthews travelled to Canada with a hastily improvised programme. It was a particularly harrowing experience for Denis Matthews: as a close friend, he still felt keenly the shock of Dennis's death, and the tour was an endless barrage of questions about the whole tragic affair. The Canadians, too, felt the loss, deprived at the last moment of their first chance to hear and see **Dennis Brain** 'in the flesh'. On 23 October, the night he would have appeared as soloist with the Kitchener-Waterloo Symphony Orchestra, Ontario, the local radio station, CKCR, presented a musical tribute on their 'Concert Hour' programme. Dennis had been booked to make two appearances in Los Angeles as soloist in February 1958. Sinclair Lott stepped in and filled the engagements, but again there was a sense of being cheated by fate. Dennis's three visits, even though primarily as an orchestral player, and later his recordings, had built up for him an enormous following in the United States.

Quite apart from all the many concert engagements which had to be cancelled or altered, the recording world also found itself greatly deprived. The amount of music Dennis had recorded by the time of his death was disproportionately small in comparison with the wide range of works that he regularly performed. Many concertos still remained unrecorded, and EMI had planned to record that winter all the Haydn horn concertos (including a recently-discovered concerto for two horns) and, at long last, the Brahms op. 40 Trio. Walter Legge had intended to engage Edwin

Fischer as the pianist. Dennis had hardly begun to explore the world of chamber-music on record; the two most notable works of which no version with Dennis exists, so far as is known, are the Schubert Octet and the Beethoven Septet. Fortunately many recordings do still exist of some of the more important works either officially, in the archives of various British and continental radio stations, or unofficially, in the hands of private collectors. It is gratifying to see the list (see Appendix) but frustrating to imagine what might have been commercially available had Dennis lived even just two or three years more.

On 13 November 1957 Dennis's will was published, revealing that he left a total of £30,109 (gross), £22,178 (net): this included a £10,000 insurance policy on his lips, which he would have received had he ever been crippled too badly to be able to continue to play. A tribute to Dennis which survives to this day is the Dennis Brain Memorial Scholarship, set up in December 1957. Peter Sharp, a chartered engineer who had been a contemporary and fellow-organist of Dennis at St Paul's School, set to work to raise some money as a memorial to him. Having first assured himself that the family was not short of money, he organized a committee to establish a suitable scholarship. A notice was circulated:

> The tragic and early death of Dennis Brain has come as a great shock to musicians and music lovers throughout the world. At school Dennis Brain was very mindful of the encouragement which should be given to music making. We felt that the best memorial which could be raised to him would be a Music Scholarship at his School bearing his name in perpetuity. With the permission of his Executors we propose that a Fund be raised sufficient after investment to meet the cost of the musical education of one musician of promise during his time at the School.
>
> Contributions even as small as the cost of a gramophone record will be welcomed, and should be sent to: R. Dowsell, Esq, St Paul's School, London, W.14.
>
> We hope that our proposal will commend itself to all who would wish to honour the memory of a great musician, and at the same time furthering the cause of music at St Paul's School.

The notice was signed by seven members of the committee, who, as old Paulines associated with music, had offered their services – Peter Sharp, Ivor Davies, then the school's Director of Music,

Peter Fricker, A. N. Gilkes, then High Master of the school, T. L. Martin, who taught at the time Dennis was at St Paul's, Bernard Shore, viola player and later London County Council Schools Music Adviser, and Norman Tucker, then Director of Sadler's Wells Opera. Assisted first by Ivor Davies, then by his successor David Robinson, Peter Sharp organized a series of sixteen concerts, for which many famous artists wrote to offer their services free: among those who played were the Amadeus Quartet, Fernando Germani, Peter Pears, Benjamin Britten and Dennis's own Ensemble. Finally, Peter Sharp persuaded EMI to pass over the royalties on a record, an issue of the BBC recording made by the Ensemble in July 1957 and broadcast after Dennis's death, towards the scholarship. By May 1962 enough money had been raised to enable the scholarship to be set up and offered every other year. Two boys have held the award so far; John Harmer, an ex-chorister from St Paul's Cathedral who later went to Bangor University, and David Pincott, who went to the school from Brighton College Junior School.

Two composers expressed their emotion through their music. Humphrey Searle was writing a set of Variations and Finale for wind and strings for the Virtuoso Ensemble when he heard of Dennis's death. He dedicated the horn's variation in his new work to the memory of Dennis, and John Burden gave the first performance on 22 January 1958. Francis Poulenc was so affected by the news that he immediately set to work to write a piece for horn and piano. The result was the Elegy, a sombre work in which he tries to convey even the car accident itself in musical terms: Neill Sanders broadcast it on 8 February 1958 in the BBC Third Programme and then performed it at one of the scholarship concerts in November the same year.

During the winter Paxmans rebuilt Dennis's horn, which had been smashed in the accident, for Yvonne. As they said, the instrument would normally have been considered a complete write-off. Nevertheless, with a great deal of skill they succeeded; the only part of the instrument that was totally beyond repair was the mouthpiece, which they had to replace. Even a labour of love could not resurrect that. Dennis's car was also reconstructed. After the accident it was judged a total write-off, and while it stood in a Hatfield garage it was further damaged by a mysterious fire.

Yvonne lost track of it, but some while later it turned up, with a new registration, and at the time of writing is still in existence.

Dennis's son Tony used his father's instrument for a while and studied the horn with John Burden at Trinity College of Music, as his second study. Yvonne later bought him a new instrument since Dennis's Alexander, styled for Dennis himself, did not suit Tony. Interestingly enough, Tony's first study was the organ, which he began without ever knowing that his father had played too. At this stage it is difficult to predict what line he will pursue. His sister Sally does not intend to take up music and his cousin Roger (Leonard's son) gave up the horn after a short while. They will follow their own inclinations, and rightly so. The pressures on the 'fourth generation' of horn-players in the Brain family would be enormous. Dennis's death marked the end of an era, the like of which we shall never see again.

❧ 11 ❧

An Evaluation

Dennis once explained the technique of horn-playing to a *Time* magazine reporter: "You smile, or at least you stretch your mouth and put it up at the corners, and then you flick a hair off with the end of your tongue, a tiny hair, and that's all there is to it." Those who have ever attempted to play the horn will tell you that there is a good deal more to it than this modest remark implied, but simplicity was always the essence of both Dennis's artistry and his personality. To try to discover just what made him the greatest horn-player of all time we shall have to look behind the simple modesty and assess the various components of his genius.

There are two basic elements in the artistry of any great instrumental performer-technique and style. Style must, of course, be based upon an adequate technique, but although style without technique is impossible, technique without style is only too common. Style is an intangible, almost indefinable quality, so we will turn our attention first to technique.

The skill of the horn-player consists at its simplest of the production of sound; the quality of that sound is the immediate product of technique. An unmistakable personal tone, immediately recognizable, is an attribute shared by the very few great instrumentalists and singers of every generation. Dennis had such a tone and its *basic* quality did not change in all the twenty or so years he played. This quality depended on four main factors; the physical make-up of the player, the embouchure, the mouthpiece, and finally the instrument.

The Brain jaw formation made an important contribution to the family's horn-playing abilities. Dennis was particularly fortunate in that he inherited it more from his uncle Alfred than his father.

He had small teeth, perfectly formed, which sloped inwards (i.e. the opposite of 'rabbits' teeth') and thus produced a concave-shaped embouchure. He used a great deal of pressure, much more than Aubrey, which he was able to support with very strong lip-muscles. After a long spell of playing there was a marked indentation where the mouthpiece had been. His third, and in many ways, most vital, physical attribute was the enormous air-pressure that he could sustain. This extraordinary stamina had two effects on his playing. It meant that he could support the enormous pressure on his lips for long periods at a time. On many occasions, especially while he was in the Royal Philharmonic Orchestra, he would play an overture and then a suite or tone-poem, come out and play a concerto as soloist and then return to his place for, say, Beethoven's "Eroica" Symphony. Second, he could control his breathing to such an extent that he could play long phrases without having to take an unmusical break. He needed only two breaths, for example, to play the whole of the opening fourteen-bar solo of Schubert's "Auf dem Strom", and in the slow movement of Mozart's Fourth Horn Concerto he could avoid splitting the long phrase that leads back to the main theme. Dennis claimed to be able to sustain a perfect note for sixty seconds. This skill came from his father. Aubrey, who had outstanding breath control, once bet Harry Blech that he could sustain a note longer on the horn than Blech could on the violin. Blech, drawing out one stroke as long as possible, lost to Aubrey, who held one note for seventy-five seconds.

The strength of his lip muscles was vitally important in view of the type of mouthpiece that Dennis used. The one which his Uncle Alfred had given him in January 1945 and which he used for most of his life was very small. It was a conical-bore French type, and although Dennis experimented from time to time with the depth of mouthpiece, he never varied the diameter, which was small enough to support a silver threepenny piece. It also had a very narrow rim: such a rim cuts into the lips and can quickly tire a player, but the deep cup of the conical mouthpiece gives a purer tone quality and rounder low notes. The recent tendency has been towards a shallower cup, which facilitates high notes, a larger bore, which gives easier blowing and greater carrying-power, and a wide rim, which cushions the lips and so allows greater endurance. Many players have taken this too far: a thick rim, although giving extra support at first, rapidly kills the surface capillary blood-vessels and control is lost. Many modern textbooks also insist that the less pressure used the better, higher notes being obtained merely by altering the angle of the airstream entering the mouthpiece. This is a fine ideal, but one so often comes across players who lack accuracy of attack and brightness and incisiveness of tone for this very reason. They can play for long periods at a time without tiring, but their tone is too dull and heavy, tending towards the flat side.

Dennis produced a clear, bright tone, which tended in pitch towards the sharp side and so emphasized the brighter overtones. His choice of mouthpiece was the determining factor: this was something of a gamble against the odds of endurance and carrying power, a gamble he won by virtue of unusual physical characteristics. These same characteristics presented him with one serious obstacle: he had an embouchure 'break', that is he had to change his lip position to go from the upper register of the instrument to the very lowest. This led to difficulty in executing rapid arpeggios and widely-spaced jumps across the break. Dennis solved this in an unusual way: he altered the angle of his instrument in relation to his mouth to suit the pitch of the notes, so that when he jumped from high to low notes his head would appear to bob up and down, rolling the mouthpiece across his lips. The result brought no sense of unease to the listener: on the contrary, his low notes had a particularly fine resonance and clarity, as if he found them easiest of all. One young player once said of Dennis: "He finds difficult all the things we find difficult, but he overcomes the difficulties and makes them sound easy." While this is not strictly true—Dennis found nearly everything about the horn very easy—it is true that he seemed completely confident to the listener, as if no problem gave him the slightest apprehension, that the traditional uncertainties of the instrument held no terrors for him.

Dennis's distinctive personal tone was also the product of his choice of instrument. Until 1952 he used, almost exclusively, the same make of horn as his father, and in his formative years he absorbed Aubrey's superlative sound daily. Dennis often complained that he could never match his father's tone quality, and to an extent he was right, although those who heard both 'in the flesh' will admit that it was a close thing. When Dennis changed to the Alexander horn he had a narrow mouthpipe fitted and continued to use his old mouthpiece, preserving almost in its entirety his former tone quality. Even after the change he admitted that he had preferred the Raoux for its softer, more legato tone, partly a result of piston action, partly of the quality of old soft metal; he thought the Alexander gave even better results but was less easy to play so smoothly.

On the purely mechanical side Dennis was again superbly equipped. His skill as an organist naturally came from agile fingers, and this agility was of enormous value to his horn-playing. His execution of rapid passages was legendary: in an informal moment he could throw off the "Flight of the Bumble-Bee" better than most flautists or Paganini's "Moto Perpetuo" as skilfully as any violinist. He had euphonium springs fitted to the valves of his Raoux horn and similarly extra-strong springs to the valves of the Alexander: with strong fingers, he maintained that the speed of return of the valve was as important as the speed with which it was depressed. A particularly apt comment was by Neville Cardus: "Dennis's lips seemed to have the sensitive touch of a pianist's fingers."

So much for technique. Style is less easy to describe, let alone analyse. Suffice it to say, by way of introduction, that Dennis's playing had an instinctive rightness and reliability that was absolute. He instilled in the listener complete confidence that blemishes would not occur. He professed to have no nerves, and it is easy to agree with that, but for all his bravura and boldness his playing lacked nothing in sensitivity. His musician's ear for tone values, his acute ear for dynamics, enabled him to ascribe just the right prominence to a solo and then withdraw. This ability is one of the most delightful aspects of his artistry, happily preserved for us on many recordings. His instinctive awareness of the role of the horn in relation to the other sections of the orchestra would enable him to place a musical phrase—like the Andante of Tchaikovsky's Fifth Symphony or the beginning of the Shepherd's Hymn in Beethoven's "Pastoral" Symphony—in context; he never demanded undivided attention by brash self-advertisement. His colleague and leader of the Philharmonia, Manoug Parikian, wrote: "He was always part of the orchestra, and his playing stood out by its impeccability, and never by different phrasing, unnecessary accentuation or change of tempo." When a passage is obviously intended to rise clearly above the general harmonies, such as in the last section of Beethoven's "Eroica" Symphony, Dennis leaves the listener in no doubt, and in such passages he has a resonance and brittleness that communicates itself to the rest of the horn section. Like his father before him, Dennis always sat on the right of the horn section, away from the vibration of the tympani which affected his lips. With bell raised the sound could bounce off the wall of the concert platform when required and thus retain its brilliance and clarity. Again, Neville Cardus: "By playing proportionately in orchestras Dennis Brain made his genius felt."

Careful analysis of Dennis's sensitivity and clarity of phrasing show that it was largely achieved by discreet and judicious use of the tongue. When once asked to slur the octave solos in the second movement of Schubert's "Unfinished" Symphony, Dennis could not, or would not, do it: he conveyed the composer's intention by observing the spirit, not always the letter, of his demands, imparting to a melodic line clarity and definition without destroying its legato character. His solos, those in Tchaikovsky's Fifth Symphony, the Andante of Borodin's Second Symphony, or Ravel's Pavane, for instance, all demonstrate that slavish adherence to printed phrasing does not always produce the most effective result. Dennis bridged the gap between merely correct playing and musical poetry.

We have mentioned Dennis's agility of both tongue and fingers. The end of the Dukas *Villanelle*, or the arpeggio solos in Rossini's overture *La Cambiale di Matrimonio*, demonstrate this extraordinary nimbleness, which was nevertheless carefully controlled. It is one thing to play Paganini's Moto Perpetuo in the artists' room for fun: it is quite another to play an equally tricky solo in the company of some eighty other players on the concert platform. Speed alone is not enough; a phrase must also be musical. A staggering example of this comes in a recording of Dvořák's D minor Serenade, with the London Baroque Ensemble conducted by Karl Haas. In the Trio section of the Minuet, Dennis has a very rapid ascending scale figure (and Haas set an extremely risky speed on this recording); not only does he play it with complete dexterity, but he even has the control to phrase it, shading it away at the end. A similar example of this controlled agility could be appreciated when one listened to his favourite encore, Le Basque by Marin Marais.

His utter fearlessness let him approach high solos with the same musicality, undaunted by the terrors of exposure. The top Cs in the first movement of Mozart's B♭ Divertimento K 287 are just picked out of thin air, with exquisite poise, just as those in Handel's Second Aria for wind are attacked with aggressive confidence. Even in the first known performance of Haydn's concert trio "Pietà di Me", where one or two notes gave him some trouble, Dennis shaped his hair-raising clarino part with an outward calmness that put the listener at ease and did nothing to disturb the balance of the singers or the other instrumentalists. Sensitivity is most important when playing in chamber-music or accompanying a singer. For years his Uncle Alfred would not play the Brahms Horn Trio as he said he could not play quietly enough. Dennis made the work his own by his complete discretion, by the same awareness of ensemble that he brought to works like the Schubert Octet or the Beethoven Septet. Mention of Schubert calls to mind his 1954 Festival Hall performance of "Auf dem Strom" with Richard Lewis and Ernest Lush. Here was the perfect balance of solos played with modest self-assurance and, when accompanying the singer, all the sensitivity and flexibility of Gerald Moore.

And yet, in all his playing, Dennis sacrificed nothing of his personality; nearly everything he played bore his unmistakable hallmarks. The slight lingering on the first of a group of semi-quavers, the swagger of an impertinent solo passage, the dreamlike quality of a solo such as that at the end of *Ein Heldenleben*—one could go on. To conjure up so many moods on the French Horn, charm, serenity, tragedy, bravura, and in all this to convey to the listener one's own immense sense of enjoyment, the sheer fun of playing, this is surely the mark of genius. So much has been said about Dennis's technique and his style: the ingredient that was the catalyst of these two qualities, which made him a legend in his own lifetime and an inspiration to succeeding generations of horn-players, was his unique personality. He knew he was good, but in a quiet, unassuming way, rather like a schoolboy who happens to find he can do a trick better than his fellows and entertains them with it for sheer fun. His complete honesty, his gentleness and kindness were the products of a very clean mind. He never failed to show a genuine admiration for anyone he knew was musical. His platform manner was cool and assured—no pose, no fuss: he had won over his audience before he even put the horn to his lips. An American, after seeing Dennis play with the Scottish National Orchestra in February 1956, wrote home: "We were rather surprised at what a small person Dennis Brain is. He seemed very quiet and shy. He may be in his thirties, but he looks about nineteen." When Walter Legge described him as the best-loved player in the Philharmonia it was no exaggeration, for his unspoilt charm and modesty endeared him to all his colleagues and his talents aroused no jealousy in them. Most of them were only too happy to sit beside him and make music with him. In fact, making music was Dennis's obsession, rather than just playing the horn, and therein lies his real contribution to twentieth-century horn-playing. Not content merely to churn out endless Mozart and Strauss concertos, he constantly explored new avenues for his enthusiasm and his talents. This restlessness took him, in a career of just over twenty years, from student to conductor, from a young prodigy to one of the world's greatest instrumentalists.

In Dennis's hands the horn became an instrument to be respected and enjoyed. Respected, because he raised the obscure classics by Mozart and Haydn from rare novelties to best-sellers and then went on to draw inspired new works from many of the important composers of his day. Enjoyed, because his utter reliability enabled audiences to relax in his presence, savouring the true artistic expression that arises only from absolute mastery. Once the horn had been established as a major solo instrument, he proceeded, by his own playing and through his own wind ensemble, to explore and exploit the chamber music repertoire, again lifting well-tried classics onto a higher plane and inspiring others to add to the repertoire. Finally, having felt that he was perhaps reaching the zenith of the horn's potential, he began to conduct, and in this too he sought new ideas and new inspiration. At the time of his death several composers were at work on special compositions for chamber orchestra.

If from all that has been said the reader gains the impression that Dennis's influence was on composers alone, let him consider for a moment the large number of very talented horn-players that exists today. Except in one or two exceptional instances, this is not the result of Dennis's teaching: unlike his father, he did not pass on his abilities directly to others. Besides, his technique was, as we have seen, quite unusual in many ways and was not the ideal basis for a manual of instruction. His unique influence lay in his ability to transmit through his playing a personality that endeared young and old alike—the young because of his boyish sense of fun and zest for life, the old because of his charm and modest self-assurance. To all he was the ideal genius, unapproachable in his unique gifts but reaching out to touch the hearts of all as a friend.

Appendix: Recordings

It has often been lamented that Dennis Brain, in particular, left so little recorded evidence of his art. A study of this discography will reveal that there exist recordings, both official and unofficial, of almost the entire horn repertoire. There are notable omissions—the Schubert Octet and the Beethoven Septet perhaps above all—but posterity owes much to the record companies, broadcasting corporations and many private enthusiasts who had the foresight to glean as much as possible from countless supreme performances.

The recordings are listed by composer. Record numbers refer to the original issue; the suffix R. indicates that the recording was later re-issued. The dates of radio broadcasts refer to the date of transmission, not necessarily the date of the recording.

The following abbreviations and symbols have been used:

Q.	Quartet	RIAS	held in the archives of Berlin Radio
S.O.	Symphony Orchestra	NOS	held in the archives of Nederlands Omroep Stichting, Hilversum
cond.	Conducted by		
Ens.	Ensemble	*	in private ownership
Philh.	Philharmonia Orchestra	C, DA, DB, HMS	HMV 78 rpm record
LSO	London Symphony Orchestra	DX, L, LX, Col.	Columbia 78 rpm record
Lon. Bar. Ens.	London Baroque Ensemble	EB	Edison Bell 78 rpm record
Orch.	Orchestra	R, SW	Parlophone 78 rpm record
BBC	held in the BBC sound archives	NGS	National Gramophone Society 78 rpm record
BIRS	held in the archives of the British Institute of Recorded Sound		
		K, M	Decca 78 rpm record
B/C	Broadcast performance, source unknown	ALP, CLP	HMV long-playing record
NDR	held in the archives of North German Radio, Hamburg	33CX	Columbia long-playing record
		CCL	Pye long-playing record
SWR	held in the archives of South West German Radio, Baden-Baden	PMA, PMB	Parlophone long-playing record
		LK, LXT	Decca long-playing record
WDR	held in the archives of West German Radio, Cologne	CTL	Capitol long-playing record
		REB	BBC long-playing record

AUBREY BRAIN

Solo or Chamber Works

BACH, J. S.	Brandenburg Concerto no. 1 in F	Busch Chamber Players	LX 436–8	R.
BEETHOVEN	Septet in Eb op. 20	Lener, Q., Draper etc.	LX 109–13	
BRAHMS	Trio for violin, horn and piano	S. Dyke, Y. Bowen	NGS 65–8	
BRAHMS	Trio for violin, horn and piano	A. Busch, R. Serkin	DB 2105–8	R.
GLAZUNOV	Reverie for horn and piano	Mrs M. Brain	EB 509	
INSTRUMENTS OF THE ORCHESTRA	{ Schubert "Ave Maria" and Beethoven no. 5 / Mendelssohn Nocturne and Siegfried Call		Col 3199	
MENDELSSOHN	Nocturne *Midsummer Night's Dream*	BBC S.O.—Boult	C 1312	
MOZART	Concerto no. 2 in Eb K 417	Royal S.O.—Batten	DA 1318	
MOZART	Concerto no. 3 in Eb K 447	BBC S.O.—Boult	EB 508–9	
MOZART	Quintet for piano and wind K 452	Long, Goossens, Thurston, Alexandra	DB 3973–4	
MOZART	Divertimento in D K 334	Lener Q., Dennis Brain	NGS 121–3	
SCHUBERT	Octet in F	Lener Q., etc.	LX 841–5	
			L 2108–13	

ALFRED BRAIN

Solo or Chamber Works

Andante & Allegro (Scarlatti)	Pastorale (Pierne)	London Wind Quintet	EB 515
Kermesse Scene, Faust (Gounod)	Quintet from Act 2 Carmen	London Wind Quintet	EB 519
Pasacalle (A. Barther)	Finale to op. 57 Suite (Lefebre)	London Wind Quintet	EB 3476
HAYDN	Concerto no. 2 in D for horn and orchestra	Janssen S.O.—Janssen	CTL 7013
STRAUSS, R.	Concerto no. 1 in Eb for horn	Hollywood Bowl—Rodzinski	B/C 22.8.31 *
VILLA-LOBOS	Choros no. 4 for 3 horns and trombone	Lott, Cave, Diner	CTL 7014

ORCHESTRAL RECORDINGS by ALFRED and AUBREY BRAIN

These are obviously too numerous to list here, but as a general guide all the pre-war and some of the wartime BBC Symphony Orchestra recordings have Aubrey as first horn, as do those by the New Queen's Hall Orchestra after 1923, the Royal Albert Hall Orchestra throughout and the London Symphony Orchestra from 1924 to 1929. There will be some exceptions, particularly in the last three orchestras mentioned.

Alfred Brain may be found in Queen's Hall recordings pre-1922, also in the London Symphony; in later years his playing may be heard in most of the films made by Twentieth Century Fox from 1944 to 1952.

The only recordings in which A. E. Brain (senior) may be heard are also of the Queen's Hall Orchestra until about 1926 and with Aubrey on Edison Bell from 1920 to 1927.

M

DENNIS BRAIN

(i) Solo or Chamber Works

Composer	Work	Performers	Catalogue	
ARNELL	Serenade for 10 wind and bass	Lon. Bar. Ens.—Haas	CCL 30120	R.
BACH, C. P. E.	Sonatas for wind	Lon. Bar. Ens.—Haas	PMB 1004	
BACH, J. S.	Brandenburg Concerto no. 1 in F	Boyd Neel and Orch.	K 1541–3 (R. USA)	
BACH, J. S.	Quoniam from Mass in B minor	Philh.—Karajan	33CX1121–3	R.
BAYEUX TAPESTRY	Incidental music for BBC children's hour—(arrangements by Alec Robertson)	Theme Music / Hunting Scene	BBC 26.9.44	
BEETHOVEN	Sonata in F op. 17 for horn and piano	Denis Matthews	DX 1152–3	R.
BEETHOVEN	Sonata in F op. 17 for horn and piano	Conrad Hansen	RIAS 20.4.50	
BEETHOVEN	Sextet op. 81b for two horns, strings	Civil, English Quartet	BBC 18.2.57	
BEETHOVEN	Quintet op. 16 for piano and wind	Gieseking, Philh. wind	33CX1322	
BEETHOVEN	Quintet op. 16 for piano and wind	Britten, Brain Ens.	BBC 22.6.55	*
BEETHOVEN	Quintet op. 16 for piano and wind	Parry, Brain Ens.	BBC 24.8.57	
BEETHOVEN	Marches for wind	Lond. Bar. Ens.—Haas	R 20614	R.
BEETHOVEN	Minuets for wind and strings	Lond. Bar. Ens.—Haas	SW 8149–50	R.
BERKELEY	Trio for violin, horn and piano	Horsley, Parikian	CLP 1029	R.
BRAHMS	Part Songs op. 17 for voices, horns and harp	Del Mar, Notts Oriana Choir, Mason, Henderson	M 560–2	
BRAHMS	Trio for violin, horn and piano	Salpeter, Preedy	REB 175	
BRITTEN	Serenade for tenor, horn and strings	Pears, Neel Orch., Britten	K 1151–3	R.
BRITTEN	Serenade for tenor, horn and strings	Pears, New S.O., Goossens	LXT 2941	
BRITTEN	Serenade for tenor, horn and strings	Haefliger, RIAS, Sacher	RIAS 20.4.50	
BRITTEN	"Fire" for tenor, horn and piano	Pears, Britten	BBC 21.6.56	
BRITTEN	"So out of the dark" for tenor, horn and piano	Pears, Britten	BBC 21.6.56	

Composer	Work	Performers	Record no.	Date	
BRITTEN	Canticle "Still Falls the Rain"	Pears, Britten	BBC	22.6.55	*
BRITTEN	Canticle "Still Falls the Rain"	Pears, Britten	NOS	6.7.56	
BRITTEN	Canticle "Still Falls the Rain"	Pears, Britten	BBC	21.6.56	
CHERUBINI	Marches for wind	Lon. Bar. Ens.—Haas	R 20613		R.
COOKE	Arioso and Scherzo for horn and strings	Carter Trio etc.	BBC	3.11.56	
COOKE	Arioso and Scherzo for horn and strings	Carter Trio etc.	BBC	5.3.57	
DITTERSDORF	Partita for wind	Lon. Bar. Ens.—Haas	PMB 1008		
DUKAS	*Villanelle* for horn and piano	Gerald Moore	DB 3300		R.
DUKAS	*Villanelle* for horn and piano	Wilfred Parry	BBC	24.8.57	
DUKAS	*Villanelle* for horn and piano	Benjamin Britten	NOS	6.7.56	
DUKAS	*Villanelle* for horn and piano	Klaus Billing	RIAS	4.5.53	
DVORAK	Serenade in D minor op. 44	Lon. Bar. Ens.—Haas	R 20604–6		R.
FERGUSON	Octet for wind and strings	Griller Q., Juler, James	K 1095–7		
FRICKER	Sonata for horn and piano	Wilfred Parry	BBC	4.8.56	*
FRICKER	Wind Quintet	Brain Ens.	BBC	24.8.57	
HANDEL	Trio Overture in C for 2 clarinets, horn	Thurston, de Peyer	R 20581		
HANDEL	Arias for wind nos. 1 and 2	Lon. Bar. Ens.—Haas	R 20617		
HAYDN	Concerto no. 1 in D	BBC Midland Orch.—Wurmser	BBC	21.1.57	R.
HAYDN	Symphony no. 22 in Eb	Lon. Bar. Ens.—Haas	SW 8122–3		R.
HAYDN	Symphony no. 31 in D "Hornsignal"	Orch. cond. Westrup	HMS 76		R.
HAYDN	Notturno in C	Lon. Bar. Ens.—Haas	PMA 1013		R.
HAYDN	Divertimento in C (Feldparthie)	Lon. Bar. Ens.—Haas	PMA 1013		
HAYDN	Divertimento in G (plus Grenadier March)	Lon. Bar. Ens.—Haas	SW 8118–9		
HAYDN	Divertimento in Bb (St Anthony)	Lon. Bar. Ens.—Haas	SW 8120–1		

(i) Solo or Chamber Works

Composer	Work	Performers	Number	
HAYDN	Divertimento in F (Feldparthie)	Lon. Bar. Ens.—Haas	R 20578-9	
HAYDN	March for Prince of Wales	Lon. Bar. Ens.—Haas	R 20579	
HAYDN	Hofball Minuette	Lon. Bar. Ens.—Haas	R 20596	
HAYDN	Concert Trio "Pietà di Me"	Sutherland, Cantelo, Nilsson, cond. Mackerras	BBC 17.12.56	*
HINDEMITH	Sonata for horn and piano	Noel Mewton-Wood	BBC 28.1.53	
HINDEMITH	Sonata for horn and piano	Conrad Hansen	RIAS 20.4.50	
HINDEMITH	Sonata for horn and piano	Denis Matthews	BBC 19.7.53	*
HINDEMITH	Concerto for horn and orchestra	WDR Orch.—Keilberth	WDR 22.1.51	
HINDEMITH	Concerto for horn and orchestra	Philh.—Hindemith	33CX1591	R.
HINDEMITH	Sonata for four horns	Sanders, Chapman, Cursue	BBC 5.1.56	*
HOFFNUNG FESTIVAL 1956	(a) as organist in Arnold 'Grand Grand Overture'			
	(b) playing hosepipe in concerto by L. Mozart		33CX1406	
IBERT	Trois Pièces Brèves	Brain Ens.	33CX1687	
INSTRUMENTS OF ORCHESTRA	with Sargent—Siegfried Horn Call		C 3622	
JACOB	Concerto for horn and strings	Riddick Orch.—Riddick	BBC 3.7.51	*
JACOB	Sextet for piano and wind	Malcolm, Brain Ens.	33CX1687	
KAMINSKI	Ballade for horn and piano	Klaus Billing	RIAS 18.9.50	R.
KAY	Miniature Quartet for wind	Brain Ens.	CCL 30120	
LEWIS	Concerto for horn and strings	BBC Midland—Gentry	BBC 18.1.57	*
MALIPIERO	Dialogue no. 4 for wind quintet	Brain Ens.	BBC 24.8.57	
MARAIS	'Le Basque' for horn and piano	Wilfred Parry	REB 175	
MASCAGNI	Intermezzo from Cavalleria Rusticana (organ)	Philh.—Karajan	33CX1265	

Composer	Work	Performer	Catalogue	
MENDELSSOHN	Nocturne from *Midsummer Night's Dream*	Philh.—Kletzki	33CX1174	*
MENDELSSOHN	Nocturne from *Midsummer Night's Dream*	Philh.—Kubelik	ALP 1049	
MILHAUD	La Cheminée du roi Renée for wind	Brain Ens.	BBC 22.6.55	R.
MOZART	Concerto for horn in D K 412	Philh.—Karajan	33CX1140	R.
MOZART	Concerto for horn in Eb K 417	Philh.—Susskind	DX 1365–6	R.
MOZART	Concerto for horn in Eb K 417	Philh.—Karajan	33CX1140	
MOZART	Concerto for horn in Eb K 417	SWR Orch.—Rosbaud	SWR 6.5.53	
MOZART	Concerto for horn in Eb K 447	NDR Orch.—Schmidt-Isserstedt	NDR 7.5.54	R.
MOZART	Concerto for horn in Eb K 447	Philh.—Karajan	33CX1140	
MOZART	Concerto for horn in Eb K 447	RIAS Orch—van Kempen	RIAS 4.5.53	
MOZART	Concerto for horn in Eb K 447	SWR Orch.—Rosbaud	SWR 6.5.53	
MOZART	Concerto for horn in Eb K 495	Hallé Orch.	DX 1123–4	R.
MOZART	Concerto for horn in Eb K 495	Philh.—Karajan	33CX1140	
MOZART	Sinfonia Concertante K 297b	Philh.—Karajan	33CX1178	
MOZART	Musical Joke K 522	Philh.—Cantelli	ALP1461	R.
MOZART	Quintet for horn and strings K 407	Griller Q.	K 1138–9	
MOZART	Quintet for horn and strings K 407	Carter Trio etc.	REB 175	
MOZART	Quintet for horn and strings K 407	English Q.	BBC 18.2.57	
MOZART	Quintet for piano and wind K 452	Gieseking, Philh.	33CX1322	
MOZART	Quintet for piano and wind K 452	Horsley, Brain Ens.	CLP 1029	R.
MOZART	Quintet for piano and wind K 452	Hansen, Brain Ens.	RIAS 22.9.51	
MOZART	Serenade for wind in Eb K 375	Lon. Bar. Ens.—Haas	R 20610–2	R.
MOZART	Serenade for wind in Eb K 375	Lon. Bar. Ens.—Haas	CCL 30119	R.
MOZART	Serenade for wind in C minor K 388	Lon. Bar. Ens.—Haas	PMA 1013	R.
MOZART	Serenade for wind in C minor K 388	Lon. Bar. Ens.—Haas	CCL 30119	R.
MOZART	Divertimento in D K 131	Royal Philh.—Beecham	DB 6649–51	

(i) Solo or Chamber Works

Composer	Work	Performers	Catalogue	
MOZART	Divertimento in D K 131	London Mozart Players—Blech	LXT 2753	R.
MOZART	Divertimento in E K 166	London Wind Players—Blech	K 2225–6	
MOZART	Divertimento in Bb K 270	Brain Ens.	33CX1687	*
MOZART	Divertimento in Bb K 270	Brain Ens.	BBC 22.6.55	
MOZART	Divertimento in Bb K 287	Philh.—Karajan	33CX1511	
MOZART	Divertimento in Eb K 289 (2 movements)	Brain Ens.	HMS 80	R.
MOZART	Divertimento in D K 334	Lener Q., Aubrey Brain	LX 841–5	
SCHOEK	Concerto for horn and strings	Collegium Musicum, Sacher	Swiss R. 4.5.56	
SCHUBERT	'Auf dem Strom' for tenor, horn and piano	Pears, Mewton-Wood	BBC 28.1.53	
SCHUBERT	'Auf dem Strom' for tenor, horn and piano	Pears, Britten	NOS 6.7.56	
SCHUBERT	'Auf dem Strom' for tenor, horn and piano	Lewis, Lush	BIRS 6.4.54	
SCHUMANN	Adagio and Allegro for horn and piano	Gerald Moore	DX 1867	R.
SCHUMANN	Adagio and Allegro for horn and piano	Benjamin Britten	NOS 6.7.56	
SCHUMANN	Adagio and Allegro for horn and piano	Klaus Billing	RIAS 4.5.53	
SEIBER	Notturno for horn and strings	LSO—Cameron	BBC 29.7.55	*
SEIBER	Fantasy for flute, horn and strings	Morris, Allegri Q.	BBC 6.2.57	
STRAUSS, R.	Concerto no. 1 in Eb for horn	Philh.—Galliera	DX 1397–8	
STRAUSS, R.	Concerto no. 1 in Eb for horn	Philh.—Sawallisch	33CX1491	R.
STRAUSS, R.	Concerto no. 1 in Eb for horn	NDR Orch.—Schmidt-Isserstedt	NDR 7.5.54	
STRAUSS, R.	Concerto no. 2 in Eb for horn	BBC Welsh Orch.—Jenkins	BBC 5.2.51	*

STRAUSS, R.	Concerto no. 2 in Eb for horn	Philh.—Sawallisch	33CX1491	R.
STRAUSS, R.	Symphony for wind instruments	Lon. Bar. Ens.—Haas	PMA 1006	R.
STRAUSS, R.	Suite for wind in Bb op. 4	Lon. Bar. Ens.—Haas	CCL 30120	R.
TOMLINSON	Romance and Rondo for horn and orchestra	BBC Concert Orch.—Tomlinson	BBC 22.6.57	*
VINTER	'Hunter's Moon' for horn and orchestra	BBC Concert Orch.—Tausky	BBC 16.6.57	
WALTZES	1. Will you remember 2. Sympathy	Bob Sharples orchestra	LK 4213	

(ii) *Speech or Lecture-Recitals*

Desert Island Discs—speech links only		BBC 13.8.56
Lecture-recital on 'The Early Horn'		BBC 23.7.55

with Jacqueline Delman (soprano), Neill Sanders (horn), Haydn Orchestra
conducted by Harry Newstone

Handel:	Minuet from *Water Music*
Bach:	Cantata no. 208 'Was mir behagt' for soprano, 2 horns, continuo
Vivaldi:	Concerto in F for 2 horns
Mozart:	Concerto no. 1 in D K 412 played on 1818 Raoux hand-horn
Mozart:	Fragment from Concerto in E K 98A—first performance
Rosetti:	Finale from Concerto in Eb
Schubert:	'Auf dem Strom' for soprano, horn and piano

*

(iii) Orchestral Recordings

It is obviously impossible to list every one of the countless orchestral recordings on which Dennis Brain appeared as first horn. As a rough guide, he is almost certain to be on every Philharmonia record issued up to the end of 1958, on most Royal Philharmonic records up to the end of 1955 (except for those made during 1949), many of the National Symphony Orchestra recordings for Decca, and on some (very few) London Mozart Players, London Chamber Orchestra and New London Orchestra recordings in the late 1940s and early 1950s. There are also a few London Baroque Orchestra recordings not listed above which include Dennis as first horn.

Of great interest, however, are a few records of works which have important horn solos and just a handful of significant or historic private recordings:

BEETHOVEN	Aria from *Fidelio* 'Abscheulicher'	Schwarzkopf. Philh.—Karajan	33CX1266	
BERLIOZ	'Royal Hunt and Storm' from *Trojans*	Royal Phil.—Beecham	BBC 2.7.47	*
BRAHMS	Tragic Overture	Philh.—Toscanini	BBC 29.9.52	*
BRAHMS	Symphony nos. 1 and 2			
BRAHMS	Symphony nos. 3 and 4	Philh.—Toscanini	BBC 1.10.52	*
BRAHMS	'Haydn' Variations			
MOZART	Aria 'Per Pietà' from *Cosi*	Schwarzkopf. Philh.—Karajan	33CX1262–4	R.
MOZART	Aria 'Per Pietà' from *Cosi*	Joan Cross. Philh.—Collingwood	DX 1353	
MOZART	Aria 'Per Pietà' from *Cosi*	Jurinac, Glyndeb.—Busch	DB 21120	
STRAUSS, R.	Four Last Songs (1st performance)	Royal Albert Hall	22.5.50	*
		Flagstad, Philh.—Furtwängler		

(iv) Films

In 1952 Anvil Films, directed by Ken Cameron, made a film of Dennis Brain and Denis Matthews playing the Beethoven Horn Sonata op. 17. The film is introduced by Dennis Brain, who briefly demonstrates the differences between the modern horn and the instrument Beethoven had in mind when writing the Sonata.

Index